LIGUORI CATHOLIC BIBLE STUDY

The Gospel
of Matthew

PROCLAIMING THE MINISTRY OF JESUS

WILLIAM A. ANDERSON, DMIN, PHD

Liguori
LIGUORI, MISSOURI

Imprimi Potest:
Harry Grile, CSsR, Provincial
Denver Province, The Redemptorists

Nihil Obstat: Rev. Msgr. Kevin Michael Quirk, JCD, JV
                Censor Librorum

Imprimatur: + Michael J. Bransfield
               Bishop of Wheeling-Charleston
January 7, 2012

Published by Liguori Publications
Liguori, Missouri 63057

To order, call 800-325-9521
www.liguori.org

Library of Congress Cataloging-in-Publication Data

Anderson, William Angor, 1937-
    The Gospel of Matthew : a Scripture study and reflection / by William A. Anderson.
        p. cm. — (The Bible study series)
    ISBN 978-0-7648-2120-2
    1. Bible. N.T. Matthew—Study and teaching. I. Title.
    BS2576.A53 2012
    226.20071—dc23

                                                        2012002262

Liguori Publications, a nonprofit corporation, is an apostolate of the Redemptorists. To learn more about the Redemptorists, visit Redemptorists.com.

Printed in the United States of America
16 15 14 13 12 / 5 4 3 2 1
First Edition

Contents

NOTE: The length of each Bible section varies. Group leaders should combine sections as needed to fit the number of sessions in their program.

ACKNOWLEDGMENTS

Bible studies and reflections such as those in this current text depend on the help of others who read the manuscript and make suggestions. I am especially indebted to Sister Anne Francis Bartus, CSJ, DMin, whose vast experience and knowledge were very helpful in bringing this series to its final form.

This series is lovingly dedicated to the memory of my parents, Kathleen and Angor Anderson, in gratitude for all they have shared with all who knew them, especially with me and my siblings.

Introduction to
Liguori Catholic Bible Study

READING THE BIBLE can be daunting. It's a complex book, and many a person of goodwill has tried to read the Bible and ended up putting it down in utter confusion. It helps to have a companion, and *Liguori Catholic Bible Study* is a solid one. Over the course of this series, you'll learn about biblical messages, themes, personalities, and events and understand how the books of the Bible rose out of the need to address new situations.

Across the centuries, people of faith have asked, "Where is God in this moment?" Millions of Catholics look to the Bible for encouragement in their journey of faith. Wisdom teaches us not to undertake Bible study alone, disconnected from the Church that was given Scripture to share and treasure. When used as a source of prayer and thoughtful reflection, the Bible comes alive.

Your choice of a Bible-study program should be dictated by what you want to get out of it. One goal of *Liguori Catholic Bible Study* is to give readers greater familiarity with the Bible's structure, themes, personalities, and message. But that's not enough. This program will also teach you to use Scripture in your prayer. God's message is as compelling and urgent today as ever, but we get only part of the message when it's memorized and stuck in our heads. It's meant for the entire person—physical, emotional, and spiritual.

We're baptized into life with Christ, and we're called to live more fully with Christ today as we practice the values of justice, peace, forgiveness, and community. God's new covenant was written on the hearts of the people of Israel; we, their spiritual descendants, are loved that intimately by God today. *Liguori Catholic Bible Study* will draw you closer to God, in whose image and likeness we are fashioned.

Group and Individual Study

The *Liguori Catholic Bible Study* series is intended for group and individual study and prayer. This series gives you the tools to start a study group. Gathering two or three people in a home or announcing the meeting of a Bible-study group in a parish or community can bring surprising results. Each lesson in this series contains a section to help groups study, reflect, pray, and share biblical reflections. Each lesson also has a second section for individual study.

Many people who want to learn more about the Bible don't know where to begin. This series gives them a place to start and helps them continue until they're familiar with all the books of the Bible.

Bible study can be a lifelong project, always enriching those who wish to be faithful to God's Word. When people complete a study of the whole Bible, they can begin again, making new discoveries with each new adventure into the Word of God.

Lectio Divina (Sacred Reading)

BIBLE STUDY isn't just a matter of gaining intellectual knowledge of the Bible; it's also about gaining a greater understanding of God's love and concern for creation. The purpose of reading and knowing the Bible is to enrich our relationship with God. God loves us and gave us the Bible to illustrate that love. As Pope Benedict XVI reminds us, a study of the Bible is not only an intellectual pursuit but also a spiritual adventure that should influence our dealings with God and neighbor.

The Meaning of *Lectio Divina*

Lectio divina is a Latin expression that means "divine or sacred reading." The process for *lectio divina* consists of Scripture readings, reflection, and prayer. Many clergy, religious, and laity use *lectio divina* in their daily spiritual reading to develop a closer and more loving relationship with God. Learning about Scripture has as its purpose the living of its message, which demands a period of reflection on the Scripture passages.

Prayer and *Lectio Divina*

Prayer is a necessary element for the practice of *lectio divina*. The entire process of reading and reflecting is a prayer. It's not merely an intellectual pursuit; it's also a spiritual one. Page 14 includes an Opening Prayer for gathering one's thoughts before moving on to the passages in each section. This prayer may be used privately or in a group. For those who use the book for daily spiritual reading, the prayer for each section may be repeated each day. Some may wish to keep a journal of each day's meditation.

Pondering the Word of God

Lectio divina is the ancient Christian spiritual practice of reading the holy Scriptures with intentionality and devotion. This practice helps Christians center themselves and descend to the level of the heart to enter an inner quiet space, finding God.

This sacred reading is distinct from reading for knowledge or information, and it's more than the pious practice of spiritual reading. It is the practice of opening ourselves to the action and inspiration of the Holy Spirit. As we intentionally focus on and become present to the inner meaning of the Scripture passage, the Holy Spirit enlightens our minds and hearts. We come to the text willing to be influenced by a deeper meaning that lies within the words and thoughts we ponder.

In this space, we open ourselves to be challenged and changed by the inner meaning we experience. We approach the text in a spirit of faith and obedience as a disciple ready to be taught by the Holy Spirit. As we savor the sacred text, we let go of our usual control of how we expect God to act in our lives and surrender our hearts and consciences to the flow of the divine (*divina*) through the reading (*lectio*).

The fundamental principle of *lectio divina* leads us to understand the profound mystery of the Incarnation, "The Word became flesh," not only in history but also within us.

Praying *Lectio* Today

Before you begin, relax your body and maintain a posture of prayer (back straight, eyes shut, feet flat on the floor). Then practice these four simple actions:

1. Read a passage from Scripture or the daily Mass readings. This is known as *lectio*. (If the Word of God is read aloud, the hearers listen attentively.)

2. Pray the selected passage with attention as you listen for a specific meaning that comes to mind. Once again, the reading is listened to or silently read and reflected or meditated on. This is known as *meditatio*.

3. The exercise becomes active. Pick a word, sentence, or idea that surfaces from your consideration of the chosen text. Does the reading remind you of a person, place, or experience? If so, pray about it. Compose your thoughts and reflection into a simple word or phrase. This prayer-thought will help you remove distractions during the *lectio*. This exercise is called *oratio*.

4. In silence, with your eyes closed, quiet yourself and become conscious of your breathing. Let your thoughts, feelings, and concerns fade as you consider the selected passage in the previous step (*oratio*). If you're distracted, use your prayer word to help you return to silence. This is *contemplatio*.

This exercise can take as long as you want, but in the context of this Bible study, 10 to 20 minutes should be sufficient.

Many teachers of prayer call contemplation the prayer of resting in God, a prelude to losing oneself in the presence of God. Scripture is transformed in our hearing as we pray and allow our hearts to unite intimately with the Lord. The Word truly takes on flesh, and this time it is manifested in our flesh.

How to Use This Bible-Study Companion

THE BIBLE, along with the commentaries and reflections found in this study, will help participants become familiar with the Scripture texts and lead them to reflect more deeply on the texts' message. At the end of this study, participants will have a firm grasp of the Gospel of Matthew and realize how that gospel offers spiritual nourishment. This study is not only an intellectual adventure, it's also a spiritual one. The reflections lead participants into their own journey with the Scripture readings.

Context

When each author wrote his gospel, he didn't simply link random stories about Jesus—he placed them in a context that often stressed a message. To help readers learn about each passage in relation to those around it, each lesson begins with an overview that puts the Scripture passages into context.

Part 1—Group Study

To give participants a comprehensive study of the Gospel of Matthew, the book is divided into 10 lessons. Lesson 1 is group study only; Lessons 2 through 10 are divided into Part 1, group study; and Part 2, individual study. For example, Lesson 2 covers passages from Matthew 3—5. The study group reads and discusses only Matthew 3—4 (Part 1). Participants privately read and reflect on Matthew 5 (Part 2).

Group study may or may not include *lectio divina*. With *lectio divina*, the group meets for ninety minutes using the first format on page 12. Otherwise the group meets for one hour using the second format on page 12, and participants are urged to privately read the *lectio divina* section at the end of Part 1. It contains additional reflections on the Scripture passages studied during the group session that will take participants even further into the passages.

Part 2—Individual Study

The gospel passages not covered in Part 1 are divided into three to six shorter components, one to be studied each day. Participants who don't belong to a study group can use the lessons for private sacred reading. They may choose to reflect on one Scripture passage per day, making it possible for a clearer understanding of the Scripture passages used in their *lectio divina* (sacred reading).

A PROCESS FOR SACRED READING

Liguori Publications has designed this study to be user friendly and manageable. However, group dynamics and leaders vary. We're not trying to keep the Holy Spirit from working in your midst, thus we suggest you decide beforehand which format works best for your group. If you have limited time, you could study the Bible as a group and save prayer and reflection for personal time.

However, if your group wishes to digest and feast on sacred Scripture through both prayer and study, we recommend you spend closer to ninety minutes each week by gathering to study and pray with Scripture. *Lectio divina* (see page 7) is an ancient contemplative prayer form that moves readers from the head to the heart in meeting the Lord. We strongly suggest using this prayer form whether in individual or group study.

GROUP-STUDY FORMATS

1. Bible Study With *Lectio Divina*

About ninety minutes of group study

- ✠ Gathering and opening prayer (3–5 minutes)
- ✠ Scripture passage read aloud (5 minutes)
- ✠ Silently review the commentary and prepare to discuss it with the group (3–5 minutes)
- ✠ Discuss the Scripture passage along with the commentary and reflection (30 minutes)
- ✠ Scripture passage read aloud a second time, followed by quiet time for meditation and contemplation (5 minutes)
- ✠ Spend some time in prayer with the selected passage. Group participants will slowly read the Scripture passage a third time in silence, listening for the voice of God as they read (10–20 minutes)
- ✠ Shared reflection (10–15 minutes)
- ✠ Closing prayer (3–5 minutes)

To become acquainted with lectio divina, *see page 7.*

2. Bible Study

About one hour of group study

- ✠ Gathering and opening prayer (3–5 minutes)
- ✠ Scripture passage read aloud (5 minutes)
- ✠ Silently review the commentary and prepare to discuss it with the group (3–5 minutes)
- ✠ Discuss the Scripture passage along with the commentary and reflection (40 minutes)
- ✠ Closing prayer (3–5 minutes)

Notes to the Leader

- ✠ Bring a copy of the *New American Bible,* revised edition.
- ✠ Plan which sections will be covered each week of your Bible study.
- ✠ Read the material in advance of each session.
- ✠ Establish written ground rules. (Example: We won't keep you longer than ninety minutes; don't dominate the sharing by arguing or debating.)
- ✠ Meet in an appropriate and welcoming gathering space (church building, meeting room, house).
- ✠ Provide name tags and perhaps use a brief icebreaker for the first meeting; ask participants to introduce themselves.
- ✠ Mark the Scripture passage(s) that will be read during the session.
- ✠ Decide how you would like the Scripture to be read aloud (whether by one or multiple readers).
- ✠ Use a clock or watch.
- ✠ Provide extra Bibles (or copies of the Scripture passages) for participants who don't bring their Bible.
- ✠ Ask participants to read "Introduction: The Gospel of Matthew" (page 15) before the first session.
- ✠ Tell participants which passages to study and urge them to read the passages and commentaries before the meeting.
- ✠ If you opt to use the *lectio divina* format, familiarize yourself with this prayer form ahead of time.

Notes to Participants

- ✠ Bring a copy of the *New American Bible,* revised edition.
- ✠ Read "Introduction: The Gospel of Matthew" (page 15) before the first class.
- ✠ Read the Scripture passages and commentary before each session.
- ✠ Be prepared to share and listen respectfully. (This is not a time to debate beliefs or argue.)

Opening Prayer

Leader: O God, come to my assistance,

Response: O Lord, make haste to help me.

Leader: Glory be to the Father, and to the Son, and to the Holy Spirit...

Response: ...as it was in the beginning, is now, and ever shall be, world without end. Amen.

Leader: Christ is the vine, and we are the branches. As branches linked to Jesus, the vine, we are called to recognize that the Scriptures are always being fulfilled in our lives. It is the living Word of God living on in us. Come, Holy Spirit, fill the hearts of your faithful, and kindle in us the fire of your divine wisdom, knowledge, and love.

Response: Open our minds and hearts as we study your great love for us as shown in the Bible.

Reader: (Open your Bible to the assigned Scripture(s) and read in a paced, deliberate manner. Pause for one minute, listening for a word, phrase, or image that you may use in your *lectio divina* practice.)

Closing Prayer

Leader: Let us pray as Jesus taught us.

Response: Our Father...

Leader: Lord, inspire us with your Spirit as we study your Word in the Bible. Be with us this day and every day as we strive to know you and serve you and to love as you love. We believe that through your goodness and love, the Spirit of the Lord is truly upon us. Allow the words of the Bible, your Word, to capture us and inspire us to live as you live and to love as you love.

Response: Amen.

Leader: May the divine assistance remain with us always.

Response: In the name of the Father, and of the Son, and of the Holy Spirit. Amen.

The Gospel of Matthew

AFTER JESUS' RESURRECTION and ascension, his followers, as dedicated Jews, believed the Jewish people would soon recognize that Jesus was truly the Messiah. Jesus' followers began a movement within Judaism known as "the Way," which referred to the new way of life with the belief that Jesus was the Messiah. Within a short period of time, however, it became evident that the Jewish religious leaders were becoming agitated and even frightened by the rapid growth of this new movement. Other movements had erupted from time to time, claiming they had found the fulfillment of the Old Testament prophecies, but these soon died out as their leaders died or were killed. The *Way*, however, seemed to be a different story. Those who professed to belong to this new *Way* proclaimed that Jesus, crucified by the Roman soldiers, had been raised from the dead.

Added to the mistrust of the religious leaders for these followers of Christ was the simmering confrontation between a zealous group within Judaism and the Roman rule. These Zealots used guerrilla warfare against the Romans, ambushing small groups of Roman soldiers and thus angering the Roman government. It was time for Rome to crush the Jewish nation, and the harsh Roman reaction began around the year 65. As the year 70 approached, it became clear that the Romans would soon invade the holy city of Jerusalem. Some Zealots, who believed God was on their side, assumed they could defend the sacred city against the Romans. Many Christians, however, as followers of Jesus' message of peace, recognized the futility of fighting the Romans and fled to areas in which Christianity was flourishing, establishing communities consisting mainly of Jewish converts to Jesus Christ.

Rome invaded Jerusalem, and a horrible slaughter took place. Roman soldiers destroyed the Temple, demolished homes and synagogues, and savagely killed a large number of the inhabitants. With the destruction of Jerusalem and the Temple, Jewish ruling structures changed. A group known as the Sadducees, whose ministry centered on the Temple, ceased to exist. A group within Judaism known as the Pharisees survived, since their ministry centered not only on the Temple but on the smaller meeting places for prayer, namely, the synagogues. The surviving Pharisees, however, believed God had punished the Jewish nation for ignoring the Mosaic Law. They launched a persecution against those whom they perceived as corrupting Judaism, most notably Christians, and drove many more Jewish Christians from Jerusalem into the surrounding regions, where they set up small communities.

At Antioch, northeast of Jerusalem, Christianity was growing rapidly in a mixed society of Jews and non-Jews. Jewish Christians joined together in small communities where they preserved many of the Jewish customs and prayers from the synagogues while at the same time professing faith in Christ. These Jewish Christians could not help but notice that most of the converts to faith in Jesus came from among the Gentiles (those who were not Jewish), and they questioned why the Israelites did not recognize Jesus as the Messiah (Christ). From their knowledge of the Scriptures, the Jewish followers of Christ expected all the people of Judea to recognize the Messiah when he arrived in the person of Jesus. Instead, they found themselves rejected by the Jewish leaders for their faith in Christ. They needed answers.

Who Was Matthew?

Within one of these Jewish Christian communities, an educated Christian Jew began to gather material for instructing his community about Jesus and his message. At the time of writing his message, this Christian Jew had a copy of the Gospel of Mark, written somewhere between 65 and 70, and a later manuscript containing many of the "sayings" of Jesus, usually referred to as the Q source. With these two manuscripts in front of him and with the knowledge he gained by listening to the community to which the author of Matthew belonged, he compiled his gospel.

The problem with identifying the author of this gospel is that he did not identify himself. A later writer named Papias identified Matthew as the one who compiled the events and messages of Jesus' life. The problem with Papias's evidence is that he states the gospel was written in Hebrew, while it was actually written in Greek. It is very difficult to translate Greek into Hebrew, which indicates that the original probably was not written in Hebrew. Because one of the sources used by the author of the Gospel of Matthew comes from an undiscovered source (designated as the M source), Papias could be referring to this earlier source, which would be an oral rather than a written source. The gospel was written somewhere around the year 85, and Matthew the Apostle most likely had died many years earlier.

In the gospel attributed to Matthew, the author names Matthew as a tax collector, while Mark (2:13–17) names him as Levi. Because a tax collector named Levi in the other synoptic gospels is named Matthew in this gospel, some commentators believe that Matthew was actually the tax collector. The problem with this argument lies in the fact that Matthew used the Gospel of Mark as a source for the story, changing only the name of the tax collector. If Matthew was actually the tax collector, why did he use Mark as a source for the story? He surely would have presented other details not found in the Gospel of Mark.

Matthew writes as a Jewish Christian. The Gospel of Matthew betrays the Jewish bias of the author, who holds Jewish laws and traditions close to his heart. For Matthew, Jesus does not come to do away with the Law, but to fulfill and correctly interpret it. Matthew quotes often from the Old Testament, showing that Jesus does indeed fulfill what has been foretold, that Jesus is the one promised throughout the Old Testament. Jesus is presented as a rabbi who enters rabbinical debates with his adversaries. As a true Christian scribe, Matthew omits the names of the scribes when Jesus comes into conflict with the leaders of the people. One of the questions Matthew must answer is a concern not only of his readers but of the author himself: "Why did the Jewish nation, the Chosen People, not recognize the Messiah?"

Although we must concede that we do not know the name of the author of this gospel, we will continue to refer to him as Matthew throughout this text.

Why Did the Jewish Nation Not Recognize the Messiah?

The author of the Gospel of Matthew was aware of the questions being asked by the people in his Jewish community. What caused so many Jewish people to miss Jesus' message and fail to recognize Jesus as the Christ? Matthew often quotes from the Greek translation of the Hebrew Scriptures to show that Jesus is the fulfillment of the Jewish expectations of the Messiah. He shows that Jesus preached mainly within Judaism, making the Jewish people the center of his ministry. Matthew concludes that the people followed the leadership of their religious authorities and rejected Jesus because their leaders rejected him.

Structure of the Gospel

A close study of the Gospel of Matthew shows that it consists of a prologue (the infancy narrative), followed by five narratives with a major discourse after each, followed by an epilogue (the passion, death, and resurrection of Jesus). Throughout this book, we shall follow the structure used by Matthew.

What Are Some Characteristics of Matthew's Gospel?

Jesus as the Son of David

Matthew presents Jesus as the Son of God and the Son of David. He wishes to show that Jesus is truly the expected Messiah promised throughout the Old Testament. The title *Son of David* is considered a messianic title, but Matthew does not allow this title to portray Jesus as a kingly type. For Matthew, Jesus is the Suffering Servant, the Son of Man who will bring about salvation through his passion, death, and resurrection.

Jesus as the Son of God

Matthew also presents Jesus as the Son of God, as one who is equal to the Creator. Throughout the Old Testament, the title Son *of* God is used for saintly individuals who follow God's will in their lives. The title is also used as a reference to the nation of Israel, the Chosen People of God. When Matthew uses this term for Jesus, he is speaking of Jesus as one with God.

Because Matthew has such a high regard for Jesus both as Messiah and as Son of God, he presents Jesus in a more divine light than Mark does.

Matthew downplays the signs of weakness in Jesus and shows him to be the wise and powerful Son of God.

The Church as the New Israel

The Gospel of Matthew is also deeply concerned about the Church. Because the people of Israel rejected the call to lead all people to God, the new Israel—the Church—must perform this function. The reign of God is identified with the Church in the gospel, but it is not a total identification. The reign of God will continue throughout eternity, whereas "the Church" refers to the disciples in union with Jesus on Earth. Not all those who become members of the Church will remain faithful, but for those who do, the promise of eternal life in the reign of God stands out. Wherever Christians gather, there is the Church. A significant aspect of Matthew's message is not only that the Church is the new Israel, but that the Church is the only *true* Israel. The Church is called to live a higher level of righteousness than were the people of Israel in Old Testament times. The members of the Church are called to the twofold commandment of love of God and neighbor.

A Favorable View of Jesus' Disciples

Matthew presents the disciples in a more favorable light than Mark does. Matthew has a high respect for the companions of Jesus, and he presents them as understanding the message of Jesus, although they must struggle with it at times. Mark's presentation of Jesus' disciples shows them completely lacking in understanding, and when they eventually do understand, they still do not fully grasp what Jesus is teaching. The disciples' weaknesses are softened in Matthew's presentation.

The End of the World

Matthew also does not see the end of the world fast approaching. The theme of the Gospel of Matthew is one of waiting patiently for the day of Final Judgment and being prepared for that day. At the end of the gospel, Matthew has Jesus commission the disciples to spread his message throughout the world. This hardly implies an immediate expectation of the end.

Infancy Narratives

MATTHEW 1—2

"Behold, the virgin shall be with child and bear a son, and they shall name him Emmanuel," which means "God is with us" (1:23).

Opening Prayer (SEE PAGE 14)

Context

Only the Gospels of Matthew and Luke have accounts of the birth and infancy of Jesus. Both accounts give us a capsulated view of the ministry of Jesus and an understanding of that ministry as seen through the light of the resurrection. The early preachers of the infancy narratives drew upon the abundant treasures of the Old Testament and structured the story of Jesus' birth by rereading these texts in light of that phenomenal event of history. The result is a summary of the joys and pains of Jesus' life caught in a quick snapshot of only a few chapters. These chapters prepare us for the message that follows.

Because Matthew and Luke belonged to a storytelling culture, they shared their message in the context of a story. Some of the events found in the infancy narratives of Matthew and Luke may not have happened as depicted. When we read these narratives, we should keep in mind that it is the message that is inspired, not the manner in which it is presented. The preachers and writers give us a theological work, not a historical or scientific presentation of the life of Jesus. Because these events may not have happened as depicted is no reason to discontinue our custom of setting out the Nativity scene each Christmas. The message can be conveyed with the visible scene as well as through the writing of gospels. In a visible presentation of the Nativity scene, a great message of God's love for all of us can be told, just as the inspired message is shared with us through the infancy narratives.

PART 1: GROUP STUDY (MATTHEW 1—2)

Read aloud Matthew 1—2

1:1–17 *The genealogy of Jesus*

Matthew had a great love for his Jewish ancestry, and he naturally begins his gospel with Jesus' family tree, starting with Abraham, the father of the Israelite nation. God promised Abraham that his offspring would be as numerous as the stars. Abraham gave birth to Isaac, who in turn gave birth to Jacob. Jacob received his father's blessings and fathered twelve sons, who became the leaders of the twelve tribes of Israel. Matthew mentions that Jacob was the father of Judah and his brothers. The reason Matthew chose to name Judah and not the other brothers is that the line of David comes through Judah. Matthew continues to follow the line of Judah down to the birth of the great king of Israelite history, namely, David.

David, chosen by God to be king of the Israelite nation, established Jerusalem as the holy city. Matthew then follows the line of David to the most tragic moment in the Old Testament history of the Israelite nation, namely, the Babylonian invasion of Jerusalem. The invasion took place 587 years before Christ and involved the slaughter of many of the inhabitants and the enslavement at Babylon of a large number of the survivors. Matthew then continues the line from the period after the Babylonian captivity to the birth of Jesus the Christ.

Matthew structures the family record of Jesus in such a way that there are fourteen generations from Abraham to King David, fourteen more generations from David to the Babylonian exile, and a final fourteen generations from the Babylonian exile to Jesus, whom Matthew identifies as the Messiah. Fourteen is twice the number seven, which was considered the perfect number at the time Matthew wrote his gospel. Six generations of seven each (or three of fourteen, as Matthew has counted) leave us on the doorstep of the seventh group. Matthew omits names in the genealogy to structure his message to fit the fourteen generations in each segment. The structure indicates that we are reading a theological narrative, not a historical one. Through the use of this genealogy, Matthew is teaching that Jesus is the fulfillment of the Old Testament promises made by God from the time of Abraham to the birth of Jesus the Christ.

Matthew shows that the family line of Jesus comes to him through Joseph, the husband of Mary. Although Matthew does not tell us that Joseph was the biological father of Jesus, he does use Joseph's family line to identify Jesus' place in Israelite history. According to the custom of the day, an adopted child had the right to claim the family line of the adopting father. When Joseph accepts Mary and Jesus into his life, he also accepts Jesus into his family lineage. According to Jewish custom, the family line comes through male ancestry. Matthew centers his infancy narrative on Joseph and writes nothing about the family line of Mary. Although Matthew does name some women in his genealogy, he always mentions them in relationship to their spouses.

The genealogies found in Matthew and Luke do not agree with each other. Both writers have a different audience. Luke, who is writing for a Gentile audience, follows Jesus' family line back to Adam, while Matthew, who is writing for a Jewish-Christian audience, traces Jesus' family line back to Abraham, the father of the Israelite nation. Matthew makes special mention of David and the Babylonian invasion of Jerusalem, major memories in the history of the Jewish people.

1:18–25 The birth of Jesus

Matthew names Mary as the mother of Jesus and notes that she was found to be with child by the power of the Holy Spirit. Mary's pregnancy poses a dilemma for Joseph. According to Jewish Law, a woman who has intercourse with a man other than the one to whom she is engaged is guilty of adultery and could be stoned to death. Joseph, a just and good man who lived in perfect harmony with the Law and the will of God, now finds himself torn between two loves, his love and concern for God's Law and an equal love and concern for Mary. Rather than having Mary stoned to death, Joseph plans to put her away quietly. Relief comes to Joseph when an angel appears to him in a dream, informing him that Mary has conceived through the power of the Holy Spirit. The angel directs him to take Mary into his home as his wife.

The Joseph of Matthew's infancy narrative is reminiscent of the patriarch Joseph, one of the twelve sons of Jacob, who was a dreamer like the Joseph of the New Testament. The Joseph of ancient times was an interpreter of dreams. His brothers sold him into slavery in Egypt, where he was eventually imprisoned. Because he was later able to interpret a dream of the reigning Pharaoh, which predicted seven years of plenty followed by seven years of famine, the Pharaoh freed Joseph from prison and placed him second in power in Egypt. This allowed Joseph to gather and store supplies during the first seven years to provide for the people during the second seven years. In the midst of the famine during the second seven years, Egypt alone enjoyed an abundance of food. At this time, Joseph brought his entire family to Egypt. Like Joseph, the son of Jacob, Joseph, the husband of Mary, receives directions in his dreams. An angel of the Lord who spoke to Joseph in his dream was often used in Scripture as a messenger sent by God.

When the angel tells Joseph that Mary is pregnant through the power of the Holy Spirit, the angel adds that she will have a son whom Joseph is to name Jesus, which means "God saves." In Jesus' era, a name given to a child often conveyed a message about the child. Although God chooses the name, the right to name the child belongs by tradition to the father. The angel recognizes Joseph's privileged position in adopting the child. The angel significantly addresses Joseph as a son of David to remind the reader again that the proper line of the Messiah is being established. The fact that no one in the Davidic line had been given the name Jesus shows that Jesus is different from the others. The virgin birth also highlights this difference.

Matthew views the birth of Jesus as the fulfillment of an Old Testament prophecy of Isaiah (7:14), which announced that a virgin would conceive a son and he would receive the name Emmanuel, which means "God is with us." The words of Isaiah came from a historical situation in Israel when Ahaz, a ruler of the northern kingdom of Israel, planned to join forces with the Assyrians in a fight against their powerful neighbors. The prophet Elijah, speaking for God, became irritated with Ahaz and informed him that a maiden would conceive and bear a child and that he would be called Emmanuel as a sign that God was with them. The child would prove that God does not need outside support but would continue to be with the people by raising up others to follow in the line of Ahaz. Matthew, who believes that everything in the Old Testament refers to Jesus, applies the title Emmanuel in Isaiah to Jesus. The birth of Jesus proclaims to the world that "God is with us." Near the end of Matthew's Gospel, we read that Jesus promises to be with us until the end of time. Even beyond the end of his earthly life, he will continue to live as *Emmanuel, God with us.*

When Joseph awakens after receiving a message in a dream, he follows the command of the angel and takes Mary as his wife. Matthew writes that Joseph had no marital relations with her "until" she gave birth to Jesus. Scholars debate the meaning of the word *until,* stressing that it does not necessarily mean he had relations with her after the birth of Jesus.

2:1–12 The visit of the Magi

Both Matthew and Luke set the birth of Jesus in Bethlehem, the town most commentators accept as the actual birthplace of Jesus. Matthew is careful to identify the location as Bethlehem of Judea as opposed to another Bethlehem found in Galilee. In Luke's infancy narrative, Mary and Joseph live in Nazareth and must travel to Bethlehem due to the taking of a census. In Matthew's narrative, the family of Jesus presumably already lives in Bethlehem at the time of Jesus' birth.

Meanwhile, some pagan astrologers, known as the Magi because of their vast knowledge, arrive in Jerusalem, the center of Judaism, searching for the newborn "king of the Jews." The only other time the title of king is used for Jesus outside of the infancy narrative comes later in Matthew's Passion narrative. Matthew links the birth of Jesus with Jesus' passion and death. Many pagans believed the discovery of a new star in the sky foreshadowed the birth of a new king. The pagan astrologers discover a new star and begin their journey to Jerusalem, seeking to know where this newborn king will be born. The image in the story of the star followed by the astrologers came from an Old Testament account in which Balaam, a pagan prophet, is forced by God to bless Israel instead of cursing the nation. While prophesying, he states that a star shall arise out of Jacob and a staff from Israel. (See Numbers 24:17.)

When King Herod hears about the birth of a newborn king, he becomes disturbed and summons the chief priests and scribes to determine where the Messiah was to be born. Matthew adds that all of Jerusalem becomes disturbed, meaning the religious leaders also become disturbed when the Magi ask where the newborn king of the Jews was to be born. The religious leaders of the Jews had no special love for Herod or for Roman rule, yet here, as during the passion of Jesus, they join an unlikely alliance with the Roman ruler concerning Jesus. The religious leaders quote from two prophets: Micah (5:1–3), who spoke of the place of the birth as Bethlehem, and 2 Samuel (5:2), who spoke of one who will shepherd the people of Israel.

Herod secretly directs the Magi to get detailed information about the child, falsely declaring that he, too, wants to pay him homage, while his real intent is to kill the child. Since the religious leaders in Jerusalem do not fulfill their role in leading the Magi to the Messiah, the star reappears now as a guiding star, and the astrologers continue their journey to the house where they find the child with Mary, his mother. Later, during the passion of Jesus, the religious leaders will again not recognize the Messiah in their midst. In Matthew's Gospel, no mention is made of Joseph, a census, or a stable, as found in Luke's Gospel.

Matthew portrays the Magi as prostrating themselves and offering homage in the same manner they would use in paying homage to God. They bring gifts to the child in accord with the ancient custom of bringing gifts to a king. The narrative does not mention the number of Magi, but does note that they bring gifts of gold, which signifies the kingship of Jesus; frankincense, which signifies the homage due Jesus; and myrrh, a burial dressing that foreshadows the death of Jesus. Many tend to believe that since the Magi brought three gifts, there must have been three of them, but the gospel doesn't mention the number of Magi who traveled to pay homage to Jesus. The Magi receive a warning in a dream not to return to Herod, so they travel to their own country by another route.

The story of the Magi foreshadows the reality that more Gentiles than Jews would eventually accept faith in Jesus as the Christ.

2:13–23 The flight into Egypt

Because Herod plans to kill the child, Joseph receives a message in a dream that he must take the child and his mother and flee to Egypt. Joseph again acts immediately when he receives a command, stealing away during the night with the child and his mother. Just as Joseph, the son of Jacob, was responsible for the Hebrew people's settling in Egypt (Genesis 45:16–20), now Joseph, the husband of Mary, brings the Holy Family to settle in Egypt until it would be safe to return to Palestine. Matthew quotes from Hosea the prophet (11:1), who stated that God called God's "son," meaning the Hebrew people, out of Egypt. Matthew applies this quotation to Jesus, whom he sees as the new Israel and the Son of God.

Herod becomes enraged when he realizes the Magi deceived him in returning home by another route, and he orders the slaughter of all the boys in Bethlehem two years old and younger. The killing of the innocents is not recorded in the history of the times, although it would not be beyond Herod to perform such an atrocious deed. About five miles north of Jerusalem, along the road to Bethlehem, is the tomb of Rachel. When the Israelites suffered under the invasion of the Babylonians, Jeremiah imagined Rachel as rising from her tomb to weep for those being led off into exile. He wrote, "In Ramah is heard the sound of sobbing, bitter weeping! Rachel mourns for her children, she refuses to be consoled for her children—they are no more!" (31:15). Matthew applies this quotation from Jeremiah to the killing of the innocents. Rachel now weeps for the death of the innocents.

An angel of the Lord appears to Joseph in a dream and informs him that those who sought Jesus' life are dead. Joseph again shows himself to be an obedient disciple by responding immediately to the command of the Lord by returning to his homeland. Matthew does not report how long the Holy Family remained in Egypt, but writes that they remained there until the death of Herod, which took place around the year 4. Matthew explains that the Holy Family settled in Nazareth instead of their hometown of Bethlehem out of fear of a notorious ruler named Archelaus, the current ruler of Bethlehem. In Luke's Gospel, Mary and Joseph return to Nazareth, which Luke presumed was their original hometown. The realization that Herod Antipas, who later put John the Baptist to death, ruled as king of the area around Nazareth should have made Joseph hesitant about settling in Nazareth. Matthew declares that this fulfilled a prophecy that Jesus would be called a Nazorean, but nowhere in the Old Testament do we find this prophecy. Matthew apparently borrows from several prophets to shape this prophecy. He does not name the source, but simply states that it was foretold by the prophets.

Review Questions

1. In which gospels do we find an account of the infancy of Jesus?
2. What is the significance of Abraham and David in the family line of Jesus?
3. What does the infancy narrative tell us about Joseph, the husband of Mary?
4. Why is Egypt so significant in the infancy narrative?
5. What historical message is expressed in the story of the Magi's following the star and paying homage to Jesus?

Closing Prayer (SEE PAGE 14)

Pray the closing prayer now or after *lectio divina.*

Lectio Divina (SEE PAGE 7)

Relax your body and maintain a posture of prayer (back straight, eyes shut, feet flat on the floor). This exercise can take as long as you want, but in the context of this Bible study, 10 to 20 minutes should be sufficient.

The meditations that follow are provided only to help group participants use this prayer form, but note that *lectio* is intended to bring one to a place of prayerful contemplation where the Word of God speaks to the hearer from his or her heart. (See page 7 for further instruction.)

The genealogy of Jesus (1:1–17)

The genealogy of Jesus shows that God had plans for the Chosen People thousands of years before the coming of Christ. Many of them lived ordinary lives with ordinary struggles, perhaps wondering what God's will was for them. Today we struggle to know God's plan in our lives. The birth of Jesus was not God's only plan for creation. Living and sharing Christ's message is part of God's plan. We have that part to live out, but like some in the genealogy, we are often unaware where we fit into God's total plan.

✠ *What can I learn from this passage?*

The birth of Jesus (1:18–25)

"I have a dream" is a famous quote from Martin Luther King, Jr. His dream was that a day would come when racism no longer existed. Many of us have dreams. The angel, a messenger from God, spoke to Joseph in his dream and left him with a difficult but rewarding message of marrying Mary and caring for Jesus. Most of us have or had a dream for our lives, and some of us were able to pursue our dream. Many dreams for the future may actually come from the Holy Spirit in our lives. The world needs laborers, doctors, teachers, homemakers, religious, and many other professions in God's plan for creation. Our dream may be to fulfill a need that benefits society in some manner. This dream may actually come from the promptings of the Holy Spirit.

✠ *What can I learn from this passage?*

The visit of the Magi (2:1–12)

In reality, Jesus did not come to die a cruel death, but in fulfilling his mission, he was destined to be crucified. He chose the dangerous path of challenging the religious leaders of his day. In our lives, we have our struggles, fears, and worries, but as we look at the life of Jesus, we are encouraged to remain faithful. Matthew, in writing his gospel, knows Jesus will die a torturous death, and he foreshadows that death in the infancy narrative, as though saying to us that Jesus lived under the shadow of the cross throughout his life. Jesus' life and death offer us great encouragement, despite what happens in our own lives.

✠ *What can I learn from this passage?*

The flight into Egypt (2:13–23)

By applying the image of God's son being called out of Egypt from the time of the Israelites to Jesus, Matthew is telling us that Jesus is reviving the journey from Egypt to the Promised Land in a manner that will correct the failure of the Israelites in their first journey from Egypt. Where the Hebrew people failed, Jesus, the new Israel, will succeed. The gospel reminds us that Jesus is not only correcting the failures of the past but also the failures of the future. Where we fail, Jesus succeeds. Through Jesus' life, death, resurrection, and ascension, he not only saves the past, he saves the future; he brings us salvation.

✠ *What can I learn from this passage?*

PART 2: INDIVIDUAL STUDY

This lesson does not have an individual-study section.

LESSON 2

Proclamation of the Reign of Heaven

MATTHEW 3—5

From that time on, Jesus began to preach and say, "Repent, for the kingdom of heaven is at hand" (4:17).

Opening Prayer (SEE PAGE 14)

Context

Part 1: Matthew 3—4 This section begins with the preaching of John the Baptist. This is followed by the role of the Spirit in Jesus' life, Jesus' temptation in the desert, and the call of his first disciples. The central message of the passage is the pronouncement by Jesus that the "kingdom of heaven" has arrived.

Part 2: Matthew 5 The author presents one of the finest-known discourses in the New Testament, namely, the Sermon on the Mount (5—7). Using the Q source, Matthew skillfully structures his gospel with the precision of a Christian scribe intent on developing a message about the demands of living in the kingdom of heaven.

PART 1: GROUP STUDY (3—4)

Read aloud Matthew 3—4

3:1-12 John the Baptist

When Matthew writes about John the Baptist, he uses Mark and Q as his sources. Those familiar with Mark's Gospel will find many similarities in Matthew's narrative. John the Baptist preaches in the desert, challenging his hearers to reform their lives because the "kingdom of heaven is at hand." Matthew, as a true Christian scribe and convert from Judaism, avoids using God's name wherever possible and speaks of the *kingdom of heaven* rather than the *kingdom of God*. When John the Baptist speaks of the kingdom of heaven, he is not speaking of eternal life, but of the presence of the kingdom here on Earth, which will reach its fulfillment in eternity.

Some commentators prefer to speak of the *reign* of heaven rather than the *kingdom* of heaven, since *kingdom* implies boundaries, whereas God's reign has no limits. Since the reign of heaven is near, John, like Jesus, calls his listeners to a radical change of life. In the person of Jesus, the reign of heaven breaks upon the world in a special and magnificent manner.

John is the one sent to prepare the way of the Lord as foretold by Isaiah. Matthew chooses a quotation from Isaiah (40:3) when he refers to John the Baptist as the one who prepares the way of the Lord. John's clothing recalls that of Elijah, an Old Testament prophet with whom John is identified, and the food is typically that of a desert sojourner. Matthew, more familiar than Mark with the geography of Judea, correctly positions the preaching of John in the desert and the baptizing at the Jordan. Mark (1:2–5) seems to have John preaching and baptizing at the same place, as though the Jordan and the desert were in the same immediate area.

When John sees Pharisees and Sadducees coming to him for baptism, he challenges them harshly, calling them a "brood of vipers." The Israelites often referred to the pagan Gentiles with the lowly and insulting name of some animal or viper. John is telling the leaders of the people they are no better than the pagan Gentiles. He challenges the religious leaders to show that they are truly repentant by their good actions. His challenge shows that not all who came to be baptized came with a sincere desire to repent. Apparently, he knew that some Pharisees and Sadducees would come for the sake of looking repentant in the eyes of others. Recognizing that some of the religious leaders believed they were chosen because they belonged to the line of Abraham, John warns that the claim to ancestry with Abraham gives them no special rights if they do not live the spirit of Abraham, adding that God could raise up descendants of Abraham from the abundance of stones found in the desert.

Throughout his gospel, Matthew uses various images for Judgment Day. In this episode, John the Baptist uses the image of an ax being laid to a root, implying that the Day of Judgment has arrived with Jesus' coming. He will bring Good News to those who accept his message and condemnation to those who reject it. Just as claiming to be descendants of Abraham is not enough, claiming to be a follower of Christ without living Christ's message is not enough. John warns his listeners that the time of separating the good (wheat) from the bad (chaff) has come. Wood and chaff were used as fuel for heat during the time of Jesus. John sees them as igniting a fire that will never end, an image of eternal condemnation.

John proclaims that his baptism is inferior to that of the One who is to come after him. Although John is referring to Jesus, he does not mention him by name. John baptizes with water, while the One who is to come will baptize with the Holy Spirit and fire. Matthew is alluding to the sacramental baptism brought to the world by Jesus. Because John recognizes the greatness of the One who is to come, he declares he is not worthy to carry his sandals.

3:13–17 The baptism of Jesus

Although Matthew spoke only of the people of Jerusalem, all Judea, and the whole region around the Jordan coming to John, he now adds that Jesus came from as far away as Galilee to be baptized by John. After the resurrection of Jesus, some followers of John during the period of the early Church believed that because he baptized Jesus, John was the greater of the two. Matthew strives to correct this misunderstanding. When John and Jesus meet, both recognize the superior position of Jesus as John declares that Jesus should baptize him. Jesus, however, responds that John should allow his baptism to fulfill all righteousness. Jesus comes to baptism, not as a sinner himself, but as one bearing the sins of all creation. He is about to begin his ministry on behalf of salvation for all people.

When Jesus comes out of the water after his baptism, he witnesses the coming of the Spirit of God in the form of a dove. The coming of the Spirit upon Jesus stands as a type of anointing. Jesus is now anointed for his ministry with the Spirit and will be guided by the Spirit throughout the rest of his life. The opening of the sky recalls an Old Testament reference from the prophet Ezekiel, who opens his book of prophecy by declaring that "the heavens opened, and I saw divine visions" (1:1). The voice from heaven recalls words from other parts of the Old Testament. (See Psalm 2:7.) In the Gospel of Mark (1:9–11), the voice from heaven addresses only Jesus, whereas the voice in the Gospel of Matthew proclaims to those around Jesus, "This is my beloved Son, with whom I am well pleased." The term *beloved Son* may be understood to mean only Son. God's being pleased with Jesus refers to his openness to the will of God. "Here is my servant whom I uphold, my chosen one with whom I am pleased. Upon him I have put my spirit; he shall bring forth justice to the nations" (Isaiah 42:1).

4:1–11 The temptation of Jesus

The influence of the Spirit in the life of Jesus is immediate, as the Spirit leads Jesus into the desert. The forty days and forty nights in the desert recall the forty years the Israelites spent in the desert during the Exodus. Where the Israelites failed, Jesus will succeed. At the baptism of Jesus, the reader learns that Jesus is the Son of God. The devil uses this identity to challenge Jesus in the first two temptations, in which the devil begins with the words, "If you are the Son of God...." The temptations become an image of the challenges Jesus will encounter during his ministry.

After forty days of fasting, the devil, recognizing that Jesus is hungry, tempts him with food. "If you are the Son of God, command that these stones become loaves of bread." This temptation recalls the journey of the Israelites in the desert and the gift of manna that they received from God. During his ministry, Jesus will take a few loaves and some fish to provide food for several thousand people, but here he rejects Satan's request by responding to the temptation with a quotation from the Book of Deuteronomy (8:3), stating that it is not physical food alone that gives nourishment, but the

Word of God. Jesus will also later state in his Sermon on the Mount that life is more than eating or drinking. The reader learns that, as important as food is, we should trust God and not make food more important in our lives than living according to God's Word.

In the second temptation, the devil takes Jesus to the highest point in the Temple and, quoting from Psalm 91 that describes divine care for God's chosen one, he challenges Jesus to show his trust in God by throwing himself off the peak of the Temple. After all, if he is the Son of God, then God will care for him. It is significant that Satan chooses the Temple for this temptation, since it is the house of God and certainly the place where God would protect those who trust in God. Jesus, however, recognizes that God is the one in control of our lives and that we cannot make God act on our behalf whenever we want or for show alone. Jesus responds with a quotation from the Book of Deuteronomy (6:16), which states that one must not put God to the test. This second encounter follows the typical form of a debate between learned rabbis. The first person would quote a Scripture text, and the other would counter it with a text that contradicts it.

Throughout his ministry, people will challenge Jesus to prove through his miracles that he is the Son of God. They will ask for a sign. Even when Jesus is on the cross, the people mock him, saying that if he is God's Son, then have God take him down from the cross. Jesus will be brought down from the cross in the glory of his resurrection, but not in the manner sought by those who view the world only in a materialistic manner.

In the final temptation, the devil takes Jesus to a high mountain and shows him all the kingdoms of the world. He promises that Jesus will have all these if he falls down and worships him. The Israelites worshiped a false image of God during their sojourn in the desert, but Jesus does not fall victim to this temptation. Where the Israelites in the desert failed, Jesus, the new Israel, succeeds in remaining faithful to the one true God. The mountain from which Jesus views the whole world is a symbolic mountain that does not really exist.

Jesus addresses the devil as Satan and harshly dismisses him with a quotation from the Book of Deuteronomy (10:20), which states that God alone is worthy of all homage. Jesus' refusal to worship the power and wealth of this world over God's reign teaches the reader that true power and wealth rest in worshiping God and not in material goods. Jesus will speak more about seeking a true eternal treasure later in Matthew's Gospel.

The power of Jesus over the devil is immediately evident as the desert of desolation becomes a plain of God's presence where angels come to minister to Jesus.

4:12–25 Jesus begins his ministry in Galilee

When Jesus hears of the arrest of John the Baptist, he moves from Nazareth to Capernaum, which will serve as the base of his ministry. Matthew informs us that this move was not done simply on the whim of Jesus. It fulfilled God's plan. Matthew quotes from the prophet Isaiah (8:21—9:1), who proclaimed that a great light would come upon the land of Zebulun and Naphtali on the road by the sea. Jesus is seen by Matthew as the great light foretold in the prophecy. The land of Capernaum is situated in the ancient area of Naphtali, but not in Zebulun. The sea originally referred to by Isaiah was the Mediterranean Sea, but Matthew changes the reference to the Sea of Galilee. The land lies in the midst of Gentile territory, but the mission of Jesus continues to be directed to the Jews. The theme of Jesus' preaching is the same as that of the Baptist in the desert. Jesus calls the people to a radical change of life because the kingdom of heaven is at hand.

It was here in Galilee that Jesus called his first disciples. The call found in the Gospel of Matthew closely follows the same episode found in the Gospel of Mark (1:16–20). Jesus calls Peter and his brother Andrew to share in his ministry of bringing the message of the kingdom to all people. Like Jesus, they will be fishers of people instead of fish. They leave their trade to follow Jesus. James and John leave their work and their family to follow Jesus. Matthew, like Mark, shows that discipleship consists of immediate and complete surrender to Jesus.

Although Jesus has settled in Capernaum, he travels throughout Galilee, where he preaches, teaches, and heals. This transition passage follows many passages found in the Gospel of Mark. Matthew alone mentions that the fame of Jesus spreads as far as Syria, the place where many believe the Gospel of Matthew was written. Great crowds from a number of areas now follow Jesus.

Review Questions

1. What message does John the Baptist preach?
2. Why does Matthew prefer the title "kingdom of heaven" to the "kingdom of God"?
3. How and why does Matthew show that Jesus is greater than John the Baptist?
4. What happens when Jesus comes out of the water after his baptism?
5. How does Jesus respond to each of the devil's three temptations in the desert?
6. What is the message behind Jesus' call of his first disciples?

Closing Prayer (SEE PAGE 14)

Pray the closing prayer now or after *lectio divina*.

Lectio Divina (SEE PAGE 7)

Relax your body and maintain a posture of prayer (back straight, eyes shut, feet flat on the floor). This exercise can take as long as you want, but in the context of this Bible study, 10 to 20 minutes should be sufficient.

The meditations that follow are provided only to help group participants use this prayer form, but note that *lectio* is intended to bring one to a place of prayerful contemplation where the Word of God speaks to the hearer from his or her heart. (See page 7 for further instruction.)

John the Baptist (3:1–12)

In the gospels, John's ministry is to prepare the way of the Lord by calling people to repentance, a change of life that will enable them to recognize the presence of Jesus in the world. When Jesus arrives and commits himself to his mission, John's main mission ends. He points to Jesus, and then slips into the background. In everything we do, we are called to point to Christ. God has given us gifts, but these gifts should not lead to boasting, but to a sincere gesture of thanking God for sharing them with us. Instead of boasting about our accomplishments, we should take an attitude that says, "Through the grace of Jesus, I can do well what I do."

✠ *What can I learn from this passage?*

The baptism of Jesus (3:13–17)

At our baptism, the struggle in our lives between the human and divine begins. In a story in the Book of Genesis, Jacob wrestles with an angel all night long and by morning begins to prevail over the angel. The angel blesses Jacob, saying, "You shall no longer be named Jacob, but Israel, because you have contended with divine and human beings and have prevailed" (32:29). This is what happens in our life. With the help of the Spirit who comes to us in a special way at our baptism, we wrestle with the human and divine throughout our lives, and we can prevail.

✠ *What can I learn from this passage?*

The temptation of Jesus (4:1–11)

Jesus endured temptations in the desert that summarized many of the temptations he would face during his ministry. Jesus was able to overcome his temptations because he never took his eye off his love of God and his mission. In the same way, we can overcome the powerful temptations in our lives if we keep our focus on Christ and the vocation God has given to us.

✠ *What can I learn from this passage?*

Jesus begins his ministry in Galilee (4:12–25)

Jesus comes as a light in the darkness, which means that he comes with a hope for salvation in a world filled with sin. As the light of the world, he wants that light to be kept burning brightly, so he chooses disciples. Today, as Christians, we are the light in the darkness. Christians are meant to be positive people, knowing that no matter how dark the world may look with all its sinfulness, the light of Christ is strongly present in the life of every baptized person. Jesus will later warn us in Matthew's Gospel not to hide that light, but to let it be seen by all.

✠ *What can I learn from this passage?*

PART 2: INDIVIDUAL STUDY (MATTHEW 5)

Day 1: The Beatitudes (5:1–12)

Matthew links together many of the sayings of Jesus and has Jesus deliver them on an unnamed mountain. Just as God gave the commandments to Moses on a mountain, so Jesus now gives the new Law to the people on a mountain. In Luke's Gospel (6:20–26), Jesus preaches the beatitudes on a plain rather than on a mountain. Luke does not have the same purpose in presenting Jesus' beatitudes. In Matthew's Gospel, Jesus speaks not only to his disciples, but to the crowd. He sits, taking the position of authority used by the great rabbis of his day. Jesus begins each of the beatitudes with the word *blessed,* which expresses a position of spiritual joy and peace for the person who practices it. The second part of the beatitude speaks of some gift in which those who practice the beatitude are already sharing.

In the first beatitude, Jesus addresses those who are poor in spirit. These are the ones who put their trust in God instead of worldly goods. Those who reach this stage of trust are already sharing in the reign of heaven, even in this life. When Luke presents Jesus' beatitudes, he speaks of those who are poor rather than those who are "poor in spirit." Matthew is speaking about a spiritual attitude, a way of thinking that affects one's manner of acting, not a social or economic condition of life as found in Luke's Gospel. In Matthew's Gospel, the call to be poor in spirit applies to those who are financially poor or rich. The poor in spirit recognize that all they have comes from God.

In the second beatitude, Jesus speaks of those who mourn. These are the ones who weep over the power of evil in the world. They mourn, not just through their tears, but through their active concern for those who are suffering in any manner. Those who practice this beatitude can find comfort in their trust of God.

In the third beatitude, Jesus states that the meek are blessed. This is not a meekness that shows weakness, but one that leads to a deeper understanding and thoughtfulness. Jesus himself, through his life and message, gives us an example of this type of meekness. He even accepts death meekly, not seeking revenge, but forgiving those who crucify him.

The land that the meek possess is the promised land of God's reign. The land was very important to the Jewish people.

In the fourth beatitude, Jesus speaks of those who hunger and thirst for righteousness. These are the ones who seek the fulfillment of God's will. They seek a world that reflects the holiness of God rather than one under the power of sin. These people have their fill in the banquet of God's love.

In the fifth beatitude, Jesus speaks about those who act with mercy. Mercy reflects the manner in which Jesus acts throughout the Gospel of Matthew, and it is not limited to those who treat us with mercy. Jesus shows mercy to all, even to those who put him to death. Those who act with mercy share in the mercy of God.

In the sixth beatitude, Jesus speaks of those who are clean of heart, which means they are of one heart with God. They live with integrity and keep their minds and hearts on the will of God. Because they are able to focus and center their lives on God, they share in the gift of truly seeing God in every aspect of life.

In the seventh beatitude, Jesus speaks of those who are peacemakers, those who bring the peace and harmony of God into the world. The original Hebrew word for peace (shalom) has a variety of meanings that cannot be translated into English with any single word. This peace includes warmth, welcome, comfort, love, and so on. Those who share this peace reflect Jesus so perfectly that they are truly sons and daughters of God.

In the eighth beatitude, Jesus addresses those who are persecuted because of their fidelity to God. Like those in the first beatitude who have abandoned all attachment to the world, those who accept persecution for God have abandoned worldly desires and share in the kingdom of heaven.

When Jesus finishes the beatitudes, he speaks directly to his listeners with the words, "Blessed are you...." Although the sentence begins with the word blessed, many commentators do not view this as one of the beatitudes, but rather as an expansion of the eighth. It is not the persecution that is important, but the motive behind accepting the persecution. Those blessed are those who are persecuted for the sake of Christ. Those who accept such persecution join the ranks of the prophets and share in the eternal reward of God's reign.

Lectio Divina

Spend 8 to 10 minutes in silent contemplation of the following passage:

When Matthew writes about the beatitudes of Jesus, he speaks about one's attitude, not one's social condition as found in the Gospel of Luke. He is actually saying the same as Paul does when he tells the Philippians to have the same attitude as found in Christ. According to the hymn found in Paul's letter, Jesus, who is God, humbled himself and took upon himself our weak, ignorant human nature. The attitude we should have is an attitude that is poor in spirit, merciful, clean of heart, peacemaking, and concern for others, all virtues we find in Christ. To practice one of the beatitudes well is to practice them all.

✠ *What can I learn from this passage?*

Day 2: Salt and Light (5:13–16)

Salt had two major uses in the time of Jesus. People used salt for seasoning and to preserve perishable food. The people of Palestine used salt from the Dead Sea, which easily lost its flavor over a period of time. Jesus tells his listeners that the disciple who has lost the true meaning of discipleship no longer has anything to offer and is as useless as salt that has lost its flavor.

Jesus addresses his listeners as the light of the world. The early Church often spoke of Jesus as the light of the world. Jesus views his audience as disciples who are called to reflect his presence on Earth. The disciples must allow their light to shine before the world, not for their own glory, but for the glory of God. The light of Christ is given to them so that others may see it.

Lectio Divina

Spend 8 to 10 minutes in silent contemplation of the following passage:

We do not have to be outstanding or powerful to be the salt of the Earth or the light of the world. However, we should be willing to live as an example of generosity and trust in God, whether we have little or much to share, whether we are active or homebound. It is not how much we share with others, but how well we share our time, talents, or treasures.

✠ *What can I learn from this passage?*

Day 3: The Old Law and the New (5:17–20)

Matthew, who has a great love for the Law, views it not only as a list of commands, but as a type of prophecy that endures because it comes from God. Like a true convert from Judaism, Matthew does not believe the old Law is ending but is, instead, reaching its fulfillment in Jesus, the perfect interpreter of the Law. Jesus teaches respect for the Law and informs his listeners that he has come to fulfill the Law, which will remain in effect until the end of the world. Those who break the Law and teach others to do so will be least in the kingdom of heaven, while those who live and teach the Law faithfully will be great in the kingdom of heaven. Jesus tells his listeners that their holiness must be greater than that of the scribes and Pharisees, whom he sees as false interpreters of the Law.

A controversy arose in the early Church concerning the traditions of the Jewish laws and whether the converts to Christ from among the Gentiles had to follow the Jewish traditions and laws. By saying that Jesus came to fulfill the Law, Matthew leaves open the door for a development that can actually appear to be a change in the Law. Matthew does not see change as a rejection of the old Law, but as a fulfillment. In the following passages, Matthew will highlight how Jesus fulfills some of the Law.

Lectio Divina

Spend 8 to 10 minutes in silent contemplation of the following passage:

Laws are necessary for the good order of society, but some laws may have to be broken for the common good, or they may be part of an exception to a law. For instance, an ambulance with a dying patient may drive through a red traffic light to get to the hospital before the patient dies. The Jews had a great love and respect for their laws, but Jesus warns them not to follow the letter of a law alone, but to understand the attitude behind it. Jesus will later sum up the Law in his command to love God, neighbor, and self. Love is the guiding principle of all laws.

✠ *What can I learn from this passage?*

Day 4: "I Say to You..." (5:21–48)

Jesus proclaims a series of six sayings known as antitheses, which consist of statements that contrast with one another. We read the expressions, "You have heard...," followed by, "I say to you...." The law is stated first, and then Jesus gives the deeper interpretation. In some cases, Jesus not only interprets the law, but even seems to change it.

The first antithesis recalls the Old Testament prohibition concerning murder. (See Exodus 20:13; Deuteronomy 5:17.) Jesus tells his listeners that anger, abusive language, and contempt for another deserve as harsh a judgment as murder; they all come from the same evil root within one's heart. The need to make amends with one's brother or sister is so great that one should set aside his or her gift at the altar to seek reconciliation with that brother or sister. To offer a gift to God without seeking some form of reconciliation seems to be a contradiction, since love of God demands love of neighbor. A second reason for seeking reconciliation is that the judgment of the courts might go against a person who could have made amends while there was still time. We should make amends with our enemies while we still have time.

In the second antithesis, Jesus reminds his listeners of the law against adultery. (See Exodus 20:14; Deuteronomy 5:18.) To look with lust on a woman means the sin has already been committed in one's heart. Avoidance of this sin should be as radical as plucking out an eye or cutting off a hand. Matthew takes his text from Mark's Gospel and implies that sins of the eye and hand are connected with sexual sins. Jesus is not calling for bodily mutilation, but for control over these gifts of sight and touch. The person with one eye or one hand can still commit sin.

The third antithesis recalls the Old Testament law concerning divorce. Jesus reminds his listeners that a decree of dismissal is allowed when a man divorces his wife. (See Deuteronomy 24:1.) Jesus recalls God's plan for marriage in which the two become one (Genesis 2:24) and warns his listeners that a man who divorces his wife actually puts her in the situation of committing adultery. Matthew adds the words "unless the marriage is unlawful" but gives no reason for this addition. Commentators have struggled with this phrase, trying to understand its meaning. Some believe it was a message to those who were converts from among the Gentiles. According to Jewish Law, a person could not marry within a certain degree of family relationship. The Gentiles did not follow this law, and as new converts, their marriage would not be considered valid if they married a relative. Not all commentators accept this interpretation.

In the fourth antithesis Jesus speaks of the prohibition against swearing falsely. (See Leviticus 19:12.) It seems Jesus is actually changing the prohibition from swearing falsely to no swearing at all. The disciples of Jesus should be so straightforward that a "yes" or "no" from them should be sufficient for a person to believe them. Because the Jews held God's name in such high esteem, they would not swear by God's name. Instead, they would call upon things touched by God, such as heaven, God's footstool, earth, or Jerusalem. Jesus points out that they are playing games when calling upon these things, because they are actually calling upon God as a witness when they do so.

In the fifth antithesis, Jesus quotes the law of retaliation. Although the law, which was an eye for an eye and a tooth for a tooth, sounds harsh, it was meant to control one's response. A person who had an eye plucked out or a tooth knocked out could only pluck out an eye or knock out a tooth in return; the punishment could not surpass the crime. (See Exodus 21:24.) Jesus goes much further than the law. He significantly states that when one strikes us on the right cheek, we should turn the other. Masters slapped their servants on the right cheek, since many were right-handed and slapped a slave on the right cheek with the back of the hand. Jesus is speaking of the worst kind of humiliating slap, and even here, the victim should follow the example of Jesus, who did not respond with revenge when the soldiers crucified him. Not only should we allow a person to take our coat, but we should offer our cloak as well. We should walk two miles with the one who forces us to walk one mile. We should not turn our back on the beggar. The attitude Jesus wishes to instill is an attitude of complete abandonment to another, that is, the attitude of giving to those in need. He is not proposing that we stand around and allow another person to hurt or abuse us.

In the sixth antithesis, Jesus quotes from the Old Testament concerning love of one's neighbor. (See Leviticus 19:18.) Nowhere do we find a command that a person should hate one's enemies, although Jewish practice at the time of Jesus was to hate those who would draw the community away from God. The Israelites looked with hatred upon the Gentiles, who threatened their national religion. Jesus urges his listeners to reject a notion that allows them to love their brothers and sisters without allowing them to love their enemies. Even tax collectors and Gentiles, some of whom do not believe in the one true God, love those who love them. Jesus rightly points out that this is part of human nature, and it takes no special merit to return love to those who love us. God, however, sends rain and sunshine upon the good and the bad. The follower of Jesus is called to practice the perfect love of God, who loves all people, friend as well as enemy, and treats them all equally. For many, this is an extremely difficult command to follow.

Lectio Divina

Spend 8 to 10 minutes in silent contemplation of the following passage:

Jesus sums up the six antitheses with his last statement, "So be perfect, just as your heavenly Father is perfect." Living as a Christian is not just a call to be holy, but to be holy and perfect as God is perfect. Jesus is fulfilling the law, which has always been directed toward love of neighbor. The call to be a disciple of Jesus is not simply a call to holiness, it is a challenge to be perfect as God is perfect, a challenge that can only be fulfilled with the help of the Holy Spirit. That help comes to us when we cultivate the habit of daily prayer.

✠ *What can I learn from this passage?*

Review Questions

1. What is the significance of Jesus' preaching his sermon on a mountain?

2. What are the beatitudes found in the Gospel of Matthew, and what is the meaning of each one (the poor in spirit, the sorrowing, the meek, those who hunger and thirst for justice, those who show mercy, the single-hearted, the peacemakers, and those who willingly suffer persecution for Jesus)?

3. What does Jesus say about anger, adultery, divorce, oaths, retaliation, and love of one's neighbor?

Signs of the Reign of Heaven

MATTHEW 6—8

Do to others whatever you would have them do to you. This is the law and the prophets (7:12).

Opening Prayer (SEE PAGE 14)

Context

Part 1: Matthew 6—7 Jesus continues to call the people to living with a spirit of trust in the arrival of the reign of heaven. Living in the reign of heaven means living with an attitude of doing all we do for God alone and not for worldly glory. God asks us to become true disciples by living as people faithful to the will of God, making God the center and treasure of our lives. Trust in God and prayerfulness are two of the virtues practiced by those living in the reign of God.

Part 2: Matthew 8 Matthew begins this book with a portrayal of Jesus as a healer and worker of great miracles as he continues his ministry in Galilee. The miracles he performs in Galilee signal the arrival of the reign of heaven. Matthew structures the first part of this book into nine neatly arranged miracles, which are further divided into three groups of three each. Between each of these groups, Matthew teaches a lesson on discipleship through the words or deeds of Jesus. The narrative section (8—9) is followed by a discourse on the mission of the disciples, which is commonly called the "Missionary Discourse of Jesus" (10—11:1), which will be treated in Lesson Four.

PART 1: GROUP STUDY (6—7)

Read aloud Matthew 6—7

6:1–18 Prayer, fasting, and almsgiving

Jesus speaks of the attitude for giving alms, praying, and fasting. These are worthy actions rewarded by God, but many using them in the wrong manner forfeit the reward. The three lessons Jesus teaches here consist of (1) actions that should be avoided, (2) the manner in which the actions should be performed, and (3) the reward that comes to those who perform these actions properly. Jesus' first concern is almsgiving. The people of Jesus' day considered almsgiving to be a necessary religious act. Most of the people of Jesus' day were poor, and many depended on these alms for their survival. The image of blowing one's horn had the same meaning in Jesus' day as in our own. Those who performed acts of almsgiving for the sake of recognition had already received the reward they sought. Those who performed these actions for God alone would receive a reward from God. God sees all actions performed in secret.

Jesus' second message concerned the proper attitude for prayer. When the time for prayer arrived, the Jews would stop what they were doing and pray, standing either in the synagogues or in the streets. Some would apparently plan their times of prayer so that they would be in a position where others would surely see and admire their appearance of holiness. They would look pious, but they would actually be hypocrites, already receiving the real reward they sought in the praise and admiration of others.

Jesus calls for secrecy in prayer and rejects the Gentile custom of multiplying prayers in an effort to chance upon a prayer that would be pleasing to God. Jesus is not speaking out against community prayer in this passage or against repeated prayers; he is simply addressing the practice of purposely praying to be admired by others. When Jesus speaks about not multiplying prayers, he is not warning against repetitious prayer, but he is calling us to have confidence in God when we pray. Although God knows our need, we tell God about the need, and then we offer God prayers of praise.

Jesus teaches us how to pray. Unlike the author of the Gospel of Luke, who begins his presentation of Jesus' prayer with "Father," Matthew has Jesus pray, "Our Father...." He emphasizes the community of the children of God who approach the Lord as one. The shorter version of this prayer found in the Gospel of Luke (11:1–4) is most likely closer to the original. The word used for "Father" in the original comes from the Hebrew *Abba,* which is a most intimate address given to God. The word must have shocked the followers of Jesus and the early converts from Judaism who would never dare to address God in so intimate a manner.

The first three petitions of the Lord's Prayer address God. When we pray that honor be given to the name of God, we are actually praying that God will always be honored. The second petition prays that God's reign will become a living reality and reach its fulfillment. The third petition prays that the will of God may be followed here on Earth with the same spirit as in heaven. In his agony in the Garden of Gethsemane, Jesus prays that God's will be done.

The next three petitions address our human needs. In the first petition, we pray for our daily bread, recognizing the providence of God and our need for God's help. The next petition recognizes the importance of reconciliation, which plays a large role in the Gospel of Matthew. Because we are sinners, we recognize our indebtedness to God's loving forgiveness. The way to gain this forgiveness is to forgive others who offend us. The final petition seeks deliverance from the test, or from temptation. In the Old Testament, the devil was not the only one to test people. God tested the faith of Abraham by asking him to sacrifice his only son. (See Genesis 22:1–18.) Only at the last moment, when Abraham proved his trust, did God keep him from performing the deed. We pray that God will not allow us to be tested beyond our strength, whether that test be from God or from the devil. Matthew returns to the theme of forgiveness and stresses that God forgives those who are willing to forgive others.

After his message about prayer, Jesus then addresses one's attitude in fasting. The hypocrite looks glum while fasting as a means of gaining the praise of others. Jesus tells his audience to appear with a clean countenance so that no one will know they are fasting and promises that God, who sees all, will reward them.

6:19–34 Trust in God

Now that Jesus has taught his followers how to pray with trust, he shows them the meaning of trust in God. Those who seek earthly riches or glory will find in them a fading treasure. Those who place their trust in heavenly treasures will find them lasting. A person decides what constitutes a treasure in life, and the heart and energies of that person will soon follow.

The people of Jesus' day believed light entered the whole body through the eye. A blind person not only lacked vision but also had darkness within. Jesus speaks of spiritual light and darkness. The person with faith will be filled with light, while the person without faith will be filled with darkness. The person who wishes to be filled with light seeks God, while the person who chooses to be filled with darkness chooses the world. No one can serve light and darkness at the same time. A person must choose one master. A disciple must make the light of Christ one's treasure in life.

In a poetic presentation of the message, Jesus speaks of living trust in God. Worry gets a person nowhere. The birds of the sky, which are not as important as human beings, are well cared for by God. How much more must God care for human creation? The flowers, without doing any work, stand out as gloriously as Solomon in all his splendor. Jesus tells his listeners not to be overly concerned about their clothing. God will provide for those who are much more important than flowers and grass, which have such a short, passing existence. The follower of Jesus must have trust in God and not be overwhelmed by the concerns of the world. The true follower of Jesus seeks God first and allows all else to follow. We must realize that Jesus is not telling us to avoid all work and planning. He is simply warning us not to place the needs of the world ahead of our desire for God. The attitude of a Christian is one of dependence on and trust in God.

7:1–12 Attitude toward others

Matthew seems to randomly place several of Jesus' sayings together in this chapter. Unlike Jesus' previous sayings, these apparently have no connection with one another. He speaks of judging others, throwing pearls before swine, a lesson on prayer, the golden rule, the narrow gate, false prophets, the true disciple, and building one's house on rock or sand. Standing at the center of these sayings is the golden rule, namely, "Do to others whatever you would have them do to you" (7:12).

Jesus teaches that a person who wishes not to be judged must not judge. Just as someone does not wish to be judged unjustly, so he or she must not judge others. Before judging another, a person should look at one's own faults and failings. The person who judges another is truly a hypocrite, since in the very act of judging, a person must overlook the log in his or her eye to see the speck in the eye of a neighbor. The failings of others stand out, while we often overlook our own failures, as great as they may be. The person with the greater fault often criticizes the one with a lesser fault.

When Jesus declares that no one should give what is holy to dogs and avoid throwing pearls before swine, he is using imagery from his own Jewish background. The Jews often referred to the Gentiles as dogs, but it is difficult to understand why Matthew placed this passage here. That which is holy or like pearls could refer to the Word of God. Perhaps Matthew is addressing some difficulty within his own community in which some are ignoring Jesus' message about judging others.

When Jesus speaks about persistent prayer, he uses an image of a son asking a parent for bread or a fish. He urges his audience to ask, seek, and knock, that is, to pray with persistence. He asks a rhetorical question, allowing his audience to answer the question in their own mind. Who would give a stone or a snake to a son who asks for bread or a fish? A serpent resembled the type of fish people ate during the time of Jesus, and a stone resembled a loaf of bread. To give someone a serpent or a stone in place of food would be the cruelest of deeds. If we know how to treat those whom we love with kindness, then how much more compassionately will God, whose love is boundless, treat us?

Although Matthew states that the golden rule sums up the Law and the prophets, it did not originate with Jesus or with Judaism. It was a common piece of wisdom accepted by most people of Jesus' time. The norms for treating others must follow the norms a person would want applied to oneself.

7:13–29 The narrow gate

Matthew ends Jesus' final discourse with a series of antitheses, contrasting those who obey the words of Jesus with those who do not. It speaks of those who pass through the narrow gate and those who do not, those who bear good fruit and those who do not, those who follow the will of God and those who do not, and those who build their faith on rock and those who do not.

In the first antithesis in this passage, Jesus states that a person can choose the narrow gate of suffering and sacrifice that leads to eternal life, or a person can choose the wider gate, as many do, that leads to damnation. In the Gospel of Luke, the author points out that few seek the narrow gate, while the author of Matthew states that few find it. In the Gospel of Matthew, the road is rough and the gate is narrow.

In the second antithesis, Jesus speaks of false prophets. During the era of the early Church, many false prophets appeared, claiming they were sharing the true message of God. Although Matthew has Jesus speaking these words here on the mountain, he could be using them as a special warning to the members of the early Church. A person can recognize true prophets by their deeds, which can be judged according to the message of Jesus' Sermon on the Mount. False prophets can be known by their unsavory fruit (evil words and deeds). In the end, they will face destruction.

In the third antithesis, Jesus speaks of discipleship. Those who profess their belief in Jesus and perform great wonders in his name are not necessarily the ones who will inherit the kingdom of heaven. Only those who live in conformity with the will of God will be recognized on Judgment Day.

Jesus ends his Sermon on the Mount with a parable, contrasting a house built on rock with a house built on sand. Those who trust in the words of Jesus build their faith on rock, while those who do not trust the words of Jesus build their faith on sand. Just as a house on sand collapses in a storm, so will the person of weak faith collapse in the moment of trial. The person with faith founded on the rock of Jesus' words will survive like the house built on rock.

Matthew announces the end of this discourse with the simple statement, "When Jesus had finished these words...." The authority of Jesus' preaching is emphasized by the amazement of the crowd. The people had grown accustomed to the scribes of the past quoting other well-known scribes. Jesus speaks on his own authority.

Review Questions

1. When Jesus speaks about almsgiving, prayer, and fasting, what central message does he teach?

2. How does the Lord's Prayer teach us to pray?

3. What is the golden rule?

4. What is a characteristic of discipleship?

5. What is the message behind the parable about the house built on rock and the one built on sand?

Closing Prayer (SEE PAGE 14)

Pray the closing prayer now or after *lectio divina*.

Lectio Divina (SEE PAGE 7)

Relax your body and maintain a posture of prayer (back straight, eyes shut, feet flat on the floor). This exercise can take as long as you want, but in the context of this Bible study, 10 to 20 minutes should be sufficient.

The meditations that follow are provided only to help group participants use this prayer form, but note that *lectio* is intended to bring one to a place of prayerful contemplation where the Word of God speaks to the hearer from his or her heart. (See page 7 for further instruction.)

Prayer, fasting, and almsgiving (6:1–18)

The Lord's Prayer contains the necessary elements of praying with a Christian attitude. In the Lord's Prayer we praise God, we seek God's help in the needs of our life, and finally we pray for forgiveness of our sins and for protection against evil temptations. When we pray for forgiveness, we add the challenging line, "as we forgive those who trespass against us." We are asking God to forgive us to the degree that we forgive others. Forgiveness of others who have sinned against us is important, and we pray for their spiritual salvation, even when we find it humanly difficult to forgive them for some hurt in our lives. Almsgiving, praying with trust, forgiveness, and fasting, all for the sake of God, is the attitude Jesus seeks to find in his disciples.

✠ *What can I learn from this passage?*

Trust in God (6:19–34)

Jesus realizes the temptations and distractions we encounter in life, but he tells us to look beyond our life to our eternal life, to store up treasures in heaven where our wealth does not fade but offers us hope of eternal joy. The allurements of the world are strong, and we can easily fall prey to the greed experienced by many, but Jesus invites us to a broader view of our life. Although we will die, we will never stop existing. By living with trust and confidence in God and building our treasure in heaven, we will die a spiritually rich person. It will be time to claim our treasure.

✠ *What can I learn from this passage?*

Attitude toward others (7:1–12)

The newspapers told the story of a woman, trapped under an overturned car, who had to lie in one position while rescuers tried to free her. A man she had never met lay on the ground in his expensive suit and held her hand for several hours, speaking to her and praying with her. Finally, when the woman was freed and put in an ambulance, she thanked the man and asked him why he'd stayed in such an uncomfortable position for so long. He answered, "I asked myself what I would want someone to do for me if I were in that situation. You know the answer." Jesus said, "Do to others whatever you would have them do to you." This is known to many as the "golden rule." It has an eternal value.

✠ *What can I learn from this passage?*

The narrow gate (7:13–29)

As true disciples, we are living stones, called to bear good fruit for God's creation. We are called to build our lives on our faith in Jesus Christ, a firm foundation. The narrow gate is a gate of love and concern for others, based on the message of love as given by Jesus. At times it will bring joy, and at other times it will demand sacrifice. As Christians, we enter through the narrow gate for love of Christ. Knowing Jesus' message is one thing, but living it is the sign of a true disciple.

✠ *What can I learn from this passage?*

PART 2: INDIVIDUAL STUDY (MATTHEW 8)

Day 1: Jesus Cures a Man With Leprosy (8:1–4)

In a transition statement from Jesus' Sermon on the Mount to the section on Jesus' miracles, Matthew writes that Jesus comes down the mountain. Matthew takes many of his miracle stories from the Gospel of Mark, although he rearranges them to teach his own specific message. The first story he takes from Mark in this section concerns the healing of a man with leprosy.

The man approaches Jesus. During the time of Jesus, leprosy included many variations of skin disorders. People with this disorder were to avoid others so as not to contaminate them. Matthew portrays the man as a person of faith who pays homage to Jesus, addresses him as "Lord," and asks for a cure if Jesus wishes to heal him. Jesus responds that he will do it, and he touches the man, an action abhorrent to the people of Jesus' day. He commands that the man be "made clean," and he is cleansed. The healing alone, however, is not enough. According to the Law of Moses, a person may be declared clean of leprosy only by the decree of a priest. Jesus shows his obedience to the Law by ordering the man to fulfill its directives and show himself to the priests. Matthew follows Mark's Gospel (1:44) by having Jesus warn the man not to tell anyone about the miracle. This story is the first of several that shows Jesus' concern for the outcasts of society.

Lectio Divina

Spend 8 to 10 minutes in silent contemplation of the following passage:

Jesus' healing of the man with leprosy not only shows Jesus' power to perform miracles; it also shows the compassion of God as expressed through Jesus, who is the image of the invisible God. God does not wish people to suffer, but suffering does happen either through some physical or some emotional misfortune. As Christians, we have the responsibility of following the example of Jesus' compassion for those with physical maladies.

✠ *What can I learn from this passage?*

Day 2: Jesus Heals a Centurion's Servant (8:5–13)

A centurion, a non-Jew, approaches Jesus with a request that Jesus cure a servant who is at home and paralyzed. When Jesus offers to go to the home of the centurion to heal his servant, the centurion shows the depth of his faith in Jesus by proclaiming that Jesus could perform the cure without going to his home. The Church uses a portion of the words of the centurion in its eucharistic celebration, namely, "Lord, I am not worthy that you should enter under my roof, but only say the word and my soul [servant] shall be healed." The centurion may have been conscious of the Jewish prohibition of a Jew's entering the home of a Gentile, thus saving Jesus some difficulty, or the centurion may have seen Jesus as a commander who could simply send out orders, knowing they would be carried out. The centurion himself had the power to rule his men from a distance.

The author of the Gospel of Matthew lived in an era in which he saw many converts to Christ coming from among the non-Jews. He expresses how amazed Jesus was at the faith of the centurion and presents Jesus' declaration that many non-Jews, together with Abraham, Isaac, and Jacob, will have a place in the kingdom of heaven. Among the Jews, the natural heirs of the kingdom, there will be some who will not share in this great gift. As a result of the faith of the centurion, Jesus sends him home with the assurance that his servant is healed.

Lectio Divina

Spend 8 to 10 minutes in silent contemplation of the following passage:

We believe we can pray for someone who may be as far away from us as halfway around the globe. The source of all prayer is faith. The centurion believed Jesus could perform this miracle without being present to his servant. The story also expresses something about the compassion of the centurion. He is not asking for a miracle for a family member, but for a slave. The story presents the centurion as a good man, worthy of a miracle for his servant.

✠ *What can I learn from this passage?*

Day 3: Healings at the Home of Peter (8:14–17)

Matthew makes some changes in the story of the cure of Peter's mother-in-law from the version found in the Gospel of Mark. In the Gospel of Mark (1:29–31), others ask Jesus to heal Peter's mother-in-law, but in Matthew's Gospel, Jesus takes the initiative. Matthew shows his respect for Peter by speaking of him as *Peter*, the name given to him by Jesus, in place of the name *Simon*, which is found in Mark's Gospel. In Matthew's Gospel, Peter's mother-in-law, freed from the fever, waits on Jesus. Mark's Gospel says she waited on "them" after the healing. Matthew could be portraying Peter's mother-in-law as a disciple called to wait on Jesus. He views disciples as those who serve others with the attitude of Christ.

Jesus expels demons and cures the sick who are brought to him. Matthew continues to show Jesus fulfilling the Old Testament prophecies. He applies a prophecy from Isaiah (53:4) concerning the suffering servant and shows how Jesus bore the infirmities and suffering of all people. In this way, Matthew identifies Jesus as the suffering servant foretold by Isaiah.

Lectio Divina

Spend 8 to 10 minutes in silent contemplation of the following passage:

In the Acts of the Apostles, we read about the conversion of Paul the Apostle. He is zealously persecuting the followers of Christ because he believes they are contaminating Judaism. On a journey to Damascus with the intention of persecuting Christians, Saul (later named Paul) falls to the ground and hears a voice that says, "Saul, Saul, why are you persecuting me?" (9:4). When Paul asks who the voice belongs to, he receives the message, "I am Jesus, whom you are persecuting" (9:5). Paul eventually recognizes that in persecuting Christians, he is actually persecuting Christ.

✠ *What can I learn from this passage?*

Day 4: The Radical Call to Discipleship (8:18–22)

Now that Matthew has presented the first set of three miracles, he changes the scene and presents a radical message on discipleship. A scribe approaches Jesus and addresses him as "Teacher" rather than "Lord." This shows that the scribe did not view Jesus as anything more than a great teacher or rabbi. The scribe is apparently sincere in his request, but Jesus warns of the difficulties in following him. Unlike the animals that have a place to rest, Jesus declares he has nowhere to rest and implies that his disciples will also lack a place to rest while on their mission. The true disciple must be willing to live without roots, ready to travel for the sake of the Gospel.

For the first time in the Gospel of Matthew, Jesus refers to himself as the "Son of Man." He apparently uses the title in place of the word *I*, but Matthew and the members of the early Church saw the more significant meaning of *messiah* in the term. They change Jesus' original meaning to a later identification of Jesus as the Messiah.

Another disciple asks Jesus to allow him to go and bury his father. The disciple is not stating that his father has just died. He is requesting that Jesus allow him to live at home *until* his father dies, at which time he will be free to follow Jesus. This disciple addresses Jesus as "Lord," which shows he has faith in the true person of Jesus. Jesus reminds him that his dedication to discipleship must be immediate and complete. When Jesus states that the disciple should let the dead bury the dead, he is referring to people who live without faith. They are spiritually dead, surrounded by worldly concerns. A true disciple does not allow worldly concerns to block his or her mission.

Lectio Divina

Spend 8 to 10 minutes in silent contemplation of the following passage:

> Saint Francis of Assisi gave up great wealth to become a poor and struggling follower of Christ. Most of us would have great difficulty living as Francis did. We realize that we can love our families and live in a warm house, but we must also recognize that we must somehow place our devotion to God at the center of our lives. Following Jesus can be a real challenge to those of us who attempt to balance an ordinary life in the world with a radical call to discipleship.

✠ *What can I learn from this passage?*

Day 5: Jesus Calms the Storm (8:23–27)

Matthew continues the theme of following Jesus as he introduces his second set of three miracles. In the first set, Matthew tells us that large crowds followed Jesus down the mountain. As we begin the second set, Matthew tells us that the disciples follow Jesus into the boat. In Mark's Gospel, the disciples enter the boat first, but Matthew has Jesus entering the boat first, followed by his disciples. For Matthew in this passage, a true disciple is one who follows Jesus.

Matthew takes the story of the storm at sea from the Gospel of Mark (4:35–41), but he shortens it and makes significant changes. A violent storm causes panic among the disciples, who call out to Jesus, who is asleep in the boat. In the Gospel of Mark, the disciples address Jesus as "Teacher" rather than "Lord," showing their weak faith. They do not ask him to save them, but to join them in their panic. In Matthew's Gospel, the disciples awaken Jesus and, addressing him as "Lord," beg him to save them. Matthew shows the disciples to be men of faith. Their faith, however, is still weak, and Jesus scolds them for their lack of faith. Jesus calms the storm by rebuking the winds and sea, bringing a great calm. Some people of Jesus' day believed evil spirits dwelt in the depths of the sea. Jesus does not just calm the storm; he rebukes the wind and the sea as though he is rebuking evil spirits. The calming of the storm stresses Jesus' divine powers, leading the amazed disciples to question who this wonderworker is.

Lectio Divina

Spend 8 to 10 minutes in silent contemplation of the following passage:

God promised to answer our prayers and calm the storms, but very often it seems God has a different answer to our prayers or no apparent answer at all. When we pray, we must believe that God never says "No." Because God is God, God may have to say, "Be patient," or, "I have a better idea in mind for you." The storm episode does not say God will answer our prayers immediately. It simply states that God is not asleep and is already preparing us for the calming of the storm.

✠ *What can I learn from this passage?*

Day 6: Jesus Casts Out Demons (8:28–34)

This story of two men who are possessed also comes from the Gospel of Mark (5:1–20), though Matthew shortens and adapts the story to fit his particular message. Matthew corrects Mark concerning the geography of Palestine. Matthew places the possessed men at Gadara, which is closer to the shore of the Sea of Galilee. Instead of one man coming out of the tombs, Matthew speaks of two men. The demons possessing these men identify Jesus as the Son of God, but Jesus does not silence them as he does in the Gospel of Mark. At the request of the demons, Jesus casts them into the swine, who rush off the cliff into the water. This action symbolically rids the land of the demons. The demons may have believed they would remain in the area if they were in the swine, but they had no idea the swine would panic and rush into the sea and drown. Many people of Jesus' day believed a stronger demon controlled weaker demons. When the swineherds reported what happened to the swine, the people of the land, fearing that Jesus is a greater demon, ask him to leave their territory.

Lectio Divina

Spend 8 to 10 minutes in silent contemplation of the following passage:

When we attempt to perform good deeds, we may encounter people who wish to cast our actions in a bad light. An important part of discipleship is to expect to be rejected, misunderstood, or accused of performing some action with an evil motive. Disciples of Jesus attempt to clear themselves against false accusations, but they remain faithful to their good actions despite the consequences. This is a difficult test for discipleship.

✠ *What can I learn from this passage?*

Review Questions

1. What messages can we get from the story of Jesus' cure of the leper?
2. Why was Jesus surprised at the faith of the centurion?
3. What is Jesus' "radical message" for discipleship?
4. How does Matthew portray the disciples' faith in the storm at sea?

Jesus' Ministry and Mission in Galilee

MATTHEW 9—11:1

Behold, I am sending you like sheep in the midst of wolves; so be shrewd as serpents and simple as doves (10:16).

Opening Prayer (SEE PAGE 14)

Context

Part 1: Matthew 9 Faith becomes a dominant theme as Jesus is able to perform miracles as a result of the faith of a man who is paralyzed, an official whose daughter has just died, a woman suffering from long-term hemorrhaging, two blind men, and a mute person. In the midst of these stories of faith, Jesus confronts those who lack faith and seek to discredit his ministry.

Part 2: Matthew 10—11:1 Jesus commissions the Twelve for ministry, giving them special gifts for their mission but warning them that they will suffer like sheep in the midst of wolves. He urges them not to fear, since he will be with them. Jesus notes that faith in him will cause division, even within families, but he urges his disciples to pick up their cross and follow his example. In following Jesus, they will receive their reward.

PART 1: GROUP STUDY (MATTHEW 9)

Read aloud Matthew 9

9:1–8 Jesus heals and forgives sin

Matthew again shortens a story found in the Gospel of Mark (2:1–12) as he presents the story of a man who is paralyzed. In the Gospel of Matthew, people bring the man before Jesus, who recognizes his faith and the faith of those around him. Matthew leaves out the details about the large crowd and the need to bring the man through the roof of the house. In leaving out these details, Matthew places the emphasis of the story on the forgiveness of sins. When Jesus forgives the man's sins, the scribes believe Jesus is blaspheming. Jesus, reading their thoughts, confronts them. The people believed that God alone could forgive sins and that the true sign of forgiveness was good health. To prove his claim, Jesus cures the paralyzed man.

In Jesus' day, people saw physical ailments as a curse from God and a sign that a person was a sinner. When Jesus forgave the man and he remained paralyzed, they mumbled that Jesus was blaspheming. When Jesus heals him, the crowd is astonished, not only at Jesus' power of healing, but at his power of forgiving sins. The people glorify God for giving such authority over sin to human beings. At the time Matthew wrote his gospel, the members of the early Church believed God had passed on this power to forgive sins to his disciples. Like those around Jesus, the people of the early Church praised God for giving such power to some of its members.

9:9–17 The call of Matthew

Matthew finishes his second series of three miracles and turns his attention to the call of Matthew, the tax collector. A man such as Matthew was considered a sinner by the Jewish people because he collected taxes for a foreign ruler, and the people suspected he overtaxed to fill his own pocket. In the Gospels of Mark (2:13) and Luke (5:27), the tax collector's name is "Levi." Matthew names the tax collector "Matthew," which is why some identify Matthew as the author of this gospel, because he alone seems to know the true name of the tax collector. When the Gospel of Matthew gives the names of the twelve apostles, the name of Matthew the tax collector is among them. The problem with identifying this Matthew as the author of the gospel lies in the question, "Why did he use Mark as a source for the story if he himself was the tax collector and would know the story firsthand?" Very few scholars accept this episode as proof that Matthew is the author of this gospel.

Jesus calls Matthew to become one of his followers, and he shares a meal with Matthew in someone's house. The author of the gospel does not tell us whose house, but since it follows the story of the call of Matthew, some commentators presume it is Matthew's house. The practice of sharing a meal was significant to the Jewish mind because it showed an intimacy and friendship between the participants. To share in a meal was to share in a person's life. The mumbling of the Pharisees is directed at the message behind Jesus' eating with tax collectors and sinners. Jesus answers that he has come not for those who are well, but for the sick, namely, the sinners. He quotes from the prophet Hosea (6:6) to show he is fulfilling the will of God, who desires mercy more than sacrifice. Jesus not only views himself sharing in the lives of sinners, but he views them as sharing in his life. The members of the early Church realized that many of those who shared at the eucharistic table were weak sinners.

When the disciples of John the Baptist ask Jesus why they and the Pharisees fast while Jesus' disciples do not, Jesus uses the image of a bridegroom as a reference to himself. People at a wedding party do not fast while the bridegroom is with them. The reference to the absence of the bridegroom refers to the death of Jesus. In this passage, the cross casts its shadow over Jesus' message. Jesus will someday leave them; then they will fast. Matthew, like Mark, could be telling the members of the early Church why they should practice fasting. Jesus warns against trying to fit the old Law into the new, and he uses the image of sewing an unshrunken cloth onto an old garment, which will cause a greater tear when the garment is washed. He also uses the image of new wine in old wineskins. The new wine will cause the old skins to burst, and the wine will be lost. Some of the converts from Judaism in the early Church tried to impose Jewish Law on the new Gentile converts. In this passage, Matthew uses the words of Jesus to offer a subtle warning against this practice.

9:18–26 The official's daughter and the woman with a hemorrhage

In this third series of three miracles, Matthew continues to make use of the healing stories found in the Gospel of Mark (5:21–43). A synagogue leader comes to Jesus with a request for a gift that is greater in the Gospel of Matthew than in that of Mark. In Matthew's version, the girl is already dead when the synagogue leader asks Jesus to come to his home. His faith is so great that he believes Jesus will raise his daughter from the dead.

On the way to the man's home, a woman who has suffered from hemorrhage for twelve years touches the tassel of Jesus' cloak, hoping to receive healing. In the Gospel of Mark, the touch alone is enough to heal her, but Matthew uses the touch as an occasion for alerting Jesus to her presence. Jesus declares that her faith has led to her healing, and at that moment she is cured.

At the home of the synagogue leader, Jesus orders the official mourners to leave and declares that the girl is asleep. The members of the early Church, because they believed in the resurrection of the dead, referred to those who had died as being "asleep in the Lord." This could be the implied message behind Jesus' words. At the touch of Jesus' hand, however, the girl rises. This statement implies resurrection. Matthew has omitted some of the details given by Mark. Jesus does not take Peter, James, and John with him, nor does he offer the girl anything to eat as he does in the Gospel of Mark.

9:27–34 Jesus heals two blind men and a mute person

Matthew speaks of two men who are blind, while Mark and Luke speak of only one. The blind men call out to Jesus using the messianic title "Son of David." Jesus tests their faith by having them follow him to the house, apparently ignoring their cry. When they ask Jesus to cure them, he again challenges their faith by asking if they believe he can do such a thing. When Jesus does cure them, the reader has no doubt the cure comes from the strong faith of the men. Matthew adds the messianic secret found in the Gospel of Mark when he tells the men to keep quiet about this incident. They ignore Jesus' request and spread word of their healing.

The curing of the person who is mute demonstrates that the Jewish people saw any type of physical ailment as a sign of demonic possession.

The reaction of those present depends on their openness to Jesus. The crowd sees this cure as a sign of God's presence among them, while the Pharisees defiantly see it as a sign of the presence of the prince of demons controlling weaker demons.

9:35–38 Workers for the harvest

Jesus travels through all the towns and villages, teaching in synagogues, preaching the Good News, and curing every kind of sickness. Matthew reveals to the reader that all of the towns had a chance to hear Jesus and to accept his message. Jesus sees the great needs of the crowd and calls upon his disciples to pray for more shepherds for the harvest. In the Old Testament, the Israelites as sheep without a shepherd is a common image.

Jesus also sees that the people are ready for "harvesting," but more disciples (laborers) are needed. Jesus tells his followers to pray that God (the harvest master) will send more laborers into the harvest. The compassion of Jesus for the people becomes more evident in this passage. This short summary serves as a transition from the narratives about healing and discipleship to the second part of this book, the "missionary discourse."

Review Questions

1. How does Jesus prove to the scribes that he can forgive sins?
2. What is the significance of the story of Matthew, the tax collector?
3. What makes the stories of the synagogue leader and the woman with the hemorrhage such important examples of great faith?
4. What is the significance of the healing of the two blind men?

Closing Prayer (SEE PAGE 14)

Pray the closing prayer now or after *lectio divina*.

Lectio Divina (SEE PAGE 7)

Relax your body and maintain a posture of prayer (back straight, eyes shut, feet flat on the floor). This exercise can take as long as you want, but in the context of this Bible study, 10 to 20 minutes should be sufficient.

The meditations that follow are provided only to help group participants use this prayer form, but note that *lectio* is intended to bring one to a place of prayerful contemplation where the Word of God speaks to the hearer from his or her heart. (See page 7 for further instruction.)

Jesus heals and forgives sin (9:1–8)

In Jesus' day, a physical healing was needed to prove that someone's sins were forgiven. In our day, we do not believe physical healing is needed to prove that a person's sins are forgiven, but we do believe God has given a very important type of healing to the Church, namely, the forgiveness of sins.

✠ *What can I learn from this passage?*

The call of Matthew (9:9–17)

Meals with Jesus often point to the Eucharist. Since Jesus ate and drank with sinners during his life, we can presume he welcomes sinners to our eucharistic celebration. In the Scriptures, sinners became followers of Christ by sharing in a meal. Sinners may also become followers of Christ when they find themselves welcomed to the eucharistic celebration.

✠ *What can I learn from this passage?*

The official's daughter
and the woman with a hemorrhage (9:18–26)

Most of us do not experience a physical touch of Christ in our lives, but we experience a faith-touch in our prayers. We believe that Jesus is with us and that he touches us through the inspiration of the Holy Spirit. When God answers our prayers, we believe God has touched our lives in some way. God does not have to use physical touch as Jesus did during his life, but we know God touches our lives in many ways.

✠ *What can I learn from this passage?*

Jesus heals two blind men and a mute person (9:27–34)

When a blind person is mentioned in the gospels, the person often represents one who is spiritually blind. A mute person often means a person who does not speak with faith. The blind men are men of faith, but Jesus seems to ignore them, forcing them to chase after him before receiving an answer to their prayer. Many people of faith can identify with these blind men. They have faith but feel like they have to chase after Jesus in their prayers. Prayer demands patience, but it also demands persistence.

✠ *What can I learn from this passage?*

Workers for the harvest (9:35–38)

The need for more shepherds in the vineyard exists today as it did in the time of Jesus. Jesus realized he needed people to preach when he saw how many hungered for his message. Jesus knows that sending shepherds into the vineyard depends on God, but he also stressed that God depends on us to recognize the need and pray for it.

✠ *What can I learn from this passage?*

PART 2: INDIVIDUAL STUDY (MATTHEW 10—11:1)

Jesus' missionary discourse forms the second part of this book in Matthew's Gospel. In this discourse, Jesus calls his disciples to take part in his mission, and he warns them that they can expect a fate no different from his.

Day 1: Choosing and Commissioning the Twelve (10:1–15)

Now that Jesus has established his power over the demons of sickness and disease, Matthew tells us that he passes this power on to his twelve disciples. In other passages in the gospel, Matthew ordinarily uses the term *disciple* more broadly, but here he restricts the term to the "twelve disciples." The gospels often refer to the twelve chosen followers of Jesus as the Twelve (capital "T"). Just as the Israelites of the Old Testament were descendants of the twelve tribes of Israel, so the followers of Jesus in the New Testament become spiritual descendants of the Twelve, who represent the new Israel. After speaking of the twelve disciples in verse one, Matthew refers to them as the twelve apostles in verse two. It is fitting for Matthew to use the term *apostle* here, since it means "one who is sent," and Jesus is sending the apostles on a mission. This is the only time Matthew uses the term *apostle* in his gospel.

Matthew offers a list of the names of the apostles that is similar to other name listings found in the New Testament. (See Mark 3:16–19, Luke 6:14–16, and Acts 1:13.) In his gospel, Matthew previously wrote about five of the disciples chosen by Jesus. The first four appeared earlier in the gospel (4:18–22), and the name of Matthew, who is mentioned in place of Levi, is referred to in the previous chapter as a tax collector (9:9). Peter is always named first in every listing of the apostles. Although Matthew does not tell us anything about the other disciples, they are apparently known well enough by the members of the early Church that Matthew does not have to explain anything more about them.

The ministry of the Twelve is to the people of Israel. After his resurrection, Jesus will direct his disciples to reach out to all nations, but at this point, Matthew presents Jesus as warning them not to visit pagan territory or enter a Samaritan town. Matthew presents Jesus' mission throughout his gospel as one directed toward the lost sheep of Israel, and he restricts his disciples to the boundaries of his own mission. They are to preach Jesus' message that the "kingdom of heaven has come near." At no cost to themselves, they received power from Jesus, and Jesus commands them to share these gifts as freely as they received them. They should travel as poor itinerants, trusting God as they travel. Matthew and Luke, unlike Mark, do not even allow them the comfort of a traveling stick or sandals. They should seek out a worthy person to live with for as long as they remain in that village. They should be ready for rejection and must trust completely in God.

When they are rejected, they should brush off the dirt of that place from their feet. In biblical times, pious Jews often shook the dust from their feet when leaving Gentile territory to show their separation from Gentile practices. When the disciples shook the dust of a Jewish house or town from their feet, it was a sign of their separation from the Jews who rejected their message about Jesus. When the Day of Judgment arrives, the fate of that place will be worse than the fate of the two notoriously sinful towns of the Old Testament, Sodom and Gomorrah.

Lectio Divina

Spend 8 to 10 minutes in silent contemplation of the following passage:

> We do not literally brush the dust off our feet today, since the gesture would have no meaning in many cultures. When we are knocked down, we simply get up and move on, recognizing that rejection often comes from ignorance rather than malice. The important form of retaliation for those of us with faith in Christ is to exhibit our faith by our words and actions.

✠ *What can I learn from this passage?*

Day 2: Persecution (10:16–33)

The disciples of Jesus can expect a fate no better than that of Jesus. Because they travel as sheep among wolves, they should have the guile of snakes to guide them. The people of Jesus' day lost many sheep to attacks by wolves. The persistence of the wolf in search of food always stood as a challenge to the cunning and ingenuity of the shepherd trying to protect his sheep. Jesus' disciples should use cunning rather than violence against their attackers. They will be dragged into pagan courts, flogged in the synagogues (which were controlled by the Pharisees of Matthew's day), brought before rulers and kings, and placed in a position where they must proclaim their faith in Jesus. When these things happen, the Holy Spirit will guide them in their witness to Jesus.

In the early days of Christianity, when some members of a family would proclaim their faith in Jesus Christ, other members of the family would often betray them to the authorities. Jesus warns the disciples that they should not unnecessarily place themselves in danger but should flee when necessary. The ministry of the disciples of Jesus will not end before the Son of Man (the resurrected Christ) comes with the New Age. This could mean the time immediately after the death and resurrection of Jesus or it could mean the Second Coming of Jesus, which many members of the early Church still expected to happen soon. Because Jesus was rejected by the leaders of the people and accused of being the prince of devils, so the disciple, who is the pupil of Jesus, should expect the same.

Jesus urges his disciples to act with courage and to continue to share his message. The day will come when everything they have to say about Jesus will be revealed and the world will know that their witness to Jesus is true. What Jesus teaches them in the hidden darkness of their private moments they are to proclaim in the light of day before all people. The power of the world can touch only the body, not the soul. If the disciples live with fear, they should fear the one who can destroy both body and soul. As far as God is concerned, they are much more valuable than the birds of the air who are well treated by God. God knows them and every hair on their head. As a result of their trust in God, they should recognize God's great concern for them and have no fear. Those who proclaim Christ before the world will find Christ acknowledging them in heaven, while the ones who deny Christ before the world will find Christ disowning them in heaven.

Lectio Divina

Spend 8 to 10 minutes in silent contemplation of the following passage:

Jesus asks us to love one another, even those who hurt us. For some, that is a type of martyrdom. Others are living with sickness, grief over the loss of a loved one, loneliness, loss of the use of a limb, paralysis, weakness from aging, or a number of other crosses in life. Suffering in this way and remaining faithful to Christ is a type of martyrdom. Faithful adherence to Christ in the midst of turmoil is a form of persecution that calls for a heroic faith.

✠ *What can I learn from this passage?*

Day 3: Family Turmoil (10:34—11:1)

The peace Jesus brings to the world is knowing one is living in accordance with God's will. In following Jesus, however, a disciple might find oneself at odds with the rest of the family. Families were the center of Jewish life, but God was even more important. Because some within the family saw faith in Jesus as a rejection of Judaism, division would occur. Some family members felt they were doing their duty to God by betraying the Christian member to the authorities. Therefore, those who chose to keep family peace and reject Christ were not worthy to be called disciples of Jesus. To be a follower of Jesus demands a willingness to suffer. The symbol of the cross was much more significant after the death and resurrection of Jesus. The word *cross* did not have the same meaning for the disciples of Jesus' day as it did for the members of the early Church for whom Matthew was writing. True disciples discover their value by losing their lives in Jesus.

The response of the people to Jesus' disciples becomes the same response they would give to Jesus himself. Those who accept the disciple, the prophet, the holy one, or a simple follower of Jesus, and treat any of them with kindness, will receive a reward for their actions. Matthew ends this book in the usual way. He tells us that Jesus has finished instructing the Twelve and that he then goes on to proclaim his message in other cities.

Lectio Divina

Spend 8 to 10 minutes in silent contemplation of the following passage:

When one takes an eternal view of life, some things that seem important become less important, and others that look less important become more important. For people of faith, it is more important to die for Christ than to preserve physical life. Jesus has an eternal view of life when he says, "Whoever finds his life will lose it, and whoever loses his life for my sake will find it."

✠ *What can I learn from this passage?*

Review Questions

1. Why is the number twelve significant in naming the disciples?
2. Why does Jesus use the image of sheep, wolves, and serpents in his message?
3. Why was there a fear that family members would betray one another?
4. What will happen to those who treat the disciples of Jesus with kindness and care?

Opposition From Israel

MATTHEW 11:2–13:53

The kingdom of heaven is like a treasure buried in a field, which a person finds and hides again, and out of joy goes and sells all that he has and buys that field (13:44).

Opening Prayer (SEE PAGE 14)

Context

Part 1: Matthew 11:2—12:50 Jesus clarifies his mission for the disciples of John the Baptist who ask if he is the "one who is to come." Jesus encounters opposition as some of the religious leaders challenge his interpretation of the Sabbath rest and accuse him of performing his miraculous deeds in the name of Beelzebul, the prince of demons. He declares that those who do the will of God in heaven are the true members of his family.

Part 2: Matthew 13:1–53 Jesus uses parables to speak of the mystery of the kingdom of heaven. His parables include stories of a sower who sows seed in a field, weeds planted among wheat, a mustard seed, yeast in wheat flour, a treasure buried in a field, the purchase of an expensive pearl, a net that catches good and bad fish, and the head of a household who brings both the old and the new from his storeroom. All the parables speak of the growth and value of the kingdom of heaven.

Part 1: Group Study (Matthew 11:2—12:50)

Read aloud Matthew 11:2—12:50

11:2–6 Jesus' testimony to John the Baptist

Although John the Baptist might not have shared all the popularly held expectations for the Messiah as the people of his time, he still did not have a clear picture of the true meaning of messiahship. When he sends his disciples to question Jesus as to whether he is the "one who is to come," he is sincerely seeking an answer for himself and his disciples. Jesus declares that he has fulfilled the expectations foretold by Isaiah, who looked toward the one who would bring healing to the afflicted (35:5–6), life to the dead (25:8), and the Good News of his message to the oppressed (61:1). The previous chapters in the Gospel of Matthew portrayed Jesus as fulfilling all these roles. Those who have expected another type of messiah should find no stumbling block in accepting Jesus, who truly fulfills the Old Testament expectations. Jesus is not only speaking of John the Baptist when he says this, but he is addressing those who will not accept him in the future. Those who accept Jesus as the "one who is to come" are called "blessed."

11:7–19 The greatness of John the Baptist

When John's messengers leave, Jesus poses two rhetorical questions to the crowd about John: Did you rush out to the desert to see some finely dressed person of royalty? Did you go out looking for something as insignificant as a reed shaking in the wind? They realize the unspoken answer to both is a resounding "no." They went to see the great prophet whose mission was to prepare the way of the Lord. He was the special messenger foretold by Malachi (3:1) in the Old Testament.

Jesus declares that John is the greatest person born of a woman, but those born into the kingdom of heaven through baptism are even greater. This message would have been lost on the audience of Jesus' day, although the readers of the Gospel of Matthew would have understood its reference to baptism.

Those who have proclaimed the reign of heaven up to this time have had to suffer some violence, such as John did who now suffered imprisonment. The people of Jesus' day believed Elijah would return immediately before the coming of the Messiah. Jesus proclaims that John the Baptist is Elijah. He does not mean that John is actually Elijah, but that he comes in the spirit of that great prophet of the Old Testament. Jesus calls his audience to listen to his words with ears of faith.

The difference between John the Baptist and Jesus becomes evident in this passage. Jesus compares his generation to children playing in the streets. Jesus came in joy, eating and drinking, and they rejected him. John came in the spirit of mourning, neither eating nor drinking, and they rejected him. Although the children of Israel were given two examples to follow, they stubbornly closed their ears to both and played their own game.

11:20–24 The unrepentant towns

Those who stubbornly refused to hear Jesus were in towns in Galilee where Jesus performed his wondrous deeds without any positive response from the people. Jesus tells the cities of Chorazin and Bethsaida that the pagan cities of Tyre and Sidon would have reformed their lives long ago if they had witnessed the miracles of Jesus. Because Chorazin and Bethsaida do not respond, it will be far worse for them on the Day of Judgment. The same holds true for the base of Jesus' operations, the city of Capernaum. Even the people of the pagan city of Sodom, the image of evil in the Old Testament, would have reformed if they had witnessed the miracles seen in Capernaum. Matthew quotes from Isaiah (14:13–15), who speaks of the false grandeur of the king of Babylon and applies this quotation to the image Capernaum had of itself. In the end, its fate will be worse than that of Sodom.

11:25–30 Knowledge of God

Jesus addresses God as "Father" in a prayer that resembles some liturgical prayers of early Christianity. He praises God for granting wisdom to the infants, a term used to refer to the early followers of Jesus. Those versed in worldly ways cannot come to the truth through human knowledge, but only through a gift from God. During Jesus' era, to say that you knew a person implied more than knowing of or about the person. Knowing someone implied a relationship. When Jesus says that no one knows the

Father except the Son, and no one knows the Son but the Father, he is stating that the Father and the Son share a deep intimacy. The Father has allowed the Son to share the revelation of truth with whomever he wishes.

The people of the Old Testament often looked upon the Law as a burden, a type of yoke used on work animals. Jesus speaks with the wisdom of the Old Testament in declaring that his yoke is "easy" and his burden "light." (See Sirach 51:23–27.) Those who love Jesus find refreshment in the wisdom he has to offer.

12:1–8 Jesus' disciples pluck grain on the Sabbath

For the Jews of Jesus' day, the Sabbath was the most sacred day of the week, a day which forbade all work and allowed only a minimum of activity. The day belonged to the Lord, and no one was to defile such a sacred day. In two stories, Jesus comes into conflict with the leaders of the people regarding this custom. In the first, Jesus' disciples pluck grain on the Sabbath, and in the second, Jesus heals on the Sabbath.

When the Pharisees see Jesus' disciples plucking grain on the Sabbath, they interpret it to be a form of work and therefore a forbidden Sabbath activity. In response to their accusation against the disciples, Jesus refers to a scene from the Old Testament in which David gave his hungry troops the temple bread to eat, even though this food was forbidden to all except the temple priest. (See 1 Samuel 21:5.) Up to this point, Matthew copied his story from Mark. Matthew inserts a second exception, saying that the temple priests must perform the sacred work of the Temple on the Sabbath, and this places the work of the Temple above the Sabbath rest. Jesus proclaims his own superiority to the Temple, a statement that must have shocked the Pharisees. Matthew gives no response from the leaders. Jesus then quotes from Hosea (6:6), reminding the Pharisees that it is mercy and not sacrifice that God wishes the people to practice. The Law is not superior to mercy, and these disciples should not be condemned for what they are doing. The final statement puts Jesus on a par with God. He proclaims he is indeed the "Lord of the Sabbath."

12:9–14 Jesus cures on the Sabbath

The second controversy occurs in a synagogue where the Pharisees ask Jesus if it is right to cure on the Sabbath. In Mark's Gospel (3:4), Jesus asks this question. Matthew mentions that a man with a shriveled hand happens to be present. Jesus, following the mode of discussion used among the rabbis of the day, answers the question by asking another. The question of whether a person could draw a sheep out of a pit on the Sabbath was a common question still being discussed among the rabbis of Jesus' day. If they can be concerned about sheep on the Sabbath, then surely they can be concerned about a human being. Jesus tells them that good deeds can certainly be performed on the Sabbath, and he heals the man with the withered hand. The reaction of the Pharisees is extreme; they now want to destroy Jesus.

12:15–21 Jesus, the chosen servant

As the cross casts its shadow across the narrative, Jesus, aware of the Pharisees' intentions, leaves that place, strongly ordering the people to keep their knowledge of his activities private. Matthew is apparently setting the scene for the prophecy from Isaiah (42:1–4) concerning Jesus' role as the suffering servant, which speaks about God's chosen one, upon whom God will place God's Spirit. Jesus has already shown himself to be God's chosen one, who has found favor with God. The Spirit of God led Jesus into the desert and guided him throughout his ministry. Because the Jews have rejected Jesus, the loving concern of God will reach out to the Gentiles through him. Despite the opposition and conflict with the leaders of the people, Jesus does not cry out. He comes, not to destroy, but to allow the Day of Judgment to reveal his true victory.

12:22–37 Jesus and Beelzebul

The curing of a man who was blind and mute becomes the source of controversy between Jesus and the Pharisees. The cure leads the people to proclaim Jesus as the Son of David, thus giving him the messianic title. Upon hearing this, the Pharisees attempt to sow doubt in the hearts of the people by accusing Jesus of casting out devils by the power of the prince of devils, known as Beelzebul. Using a short parable, Jesus points out that any kingdom set against itself will destroy itself. Among the Jews, there were some who performed healings. Jesus challenges the Pharisees to ask these people the source of their power. If, in truth, Jesus does cast out devils with the power of the Spirit of God, then the Pharisees must accept that the reign of God has broken upon the world in the person of Jesus Christ.

Jesus tells a short parable about a stronger man tying up a weaker man and robbing his house. In the same way, Jesus has bound Satan. Jesus warns the disciples that if they refuse to join with him, they will play the role of those who lead others away from him. Every blasphemy based on ignorance can be forgiven, but blasphemy that denies the activity of the Spirit of God can never be forgiven. Jesus is not declaring that God does not wish to forgive. He is telling the Pharisees that those who deny the words of the Spirit of God have closed their own minds. Because God cannot reach them, they have chosen to commit a sin no one can forgive.

Jesus shares another parable. Just as a good tree bears good fruit and a bad tree bears bad fruit, so the words and works of a person tell whether the person is good or bad. Jesus addresses the Pharisees with the same title John the Baptist used for them at the Jordan. Jesus calls them a "brood of vipers," and since they are evil, they will bear bad fruit. What a person says and does reveals much about the person, and these words and deeds will lead to acquittal or condemnation on Judgment Day.

12:38–42 The sign of Jonah

Despite the miracles they had already witnessed, the Pharisees still ask for a sign. Jesus tells them they will receive no sign but that of Jonah. Because the Pharisees have closed their minds to the words of Jesus, they do not recognize the signs they've already been given. Matthew links Jonah's three days and nights in the belly of a whale with Jesus' time in the tomb. That Jesus does not spend three nights in the tomb does not concern Matthew.

Jesus draws a further lesson from Jonah and Solomon. The people of Nineveh repented at the words of Jonah, and the Queen of Sheba came to Solomon to listen to his wisdom. (See 1 Kings 10:1–13.) The people of Nineveh and the Queen of Sheba will stand in judgment upon those who reject Jesus' words.

12:43–45 The return of the evil spirit

The desert was considered the place of unclean spirits. The people of Jesus' day must have known of exorcisms where a person received a healing, only to become worse at a later time. In a short parable, Jesus speaks about demons roaming in barren wastelands, searching for a place to rest, and eventually returning to their first place of rest, the person from whom they were expelled. On their return, they bring a more total conquest, many spirits more evil than themselves. Not only must a person turn away from evil, but that person must turn toward Jesus and his message. Jesus comes to Israel and casts out the power of evil, but the leaders of the Jews, refusing to accept Jesus, make the last state of the nation worse than the first.

12:46–50 Jesus' family and the will of God

In the midst of his preaching, the relatives of Jesus ask to speak with him. Jesus uses the occasion to teach a message about those who are truly related to him, namely, those who live according to the will of God. Jesus sets aside physical relationship for the sake of spiritual relationship, which he places on a higher plane.

Review Questions

1. Why would Jesus be a "stumbling block" for some of the people of his own day?
2. What is the significance of the fact that the Son and the Father know each other?
3. What does Jesus teach concerning the Sabbath?

Closing Prayer (SEE PAGE 14)

Pray the closing prayer now or after *lectio divina*.

Lectio Divina (SEE PAGE 7)

Relax your body and maintain a posture of prayer (back straight, eyes shut, feet flat on the floor). This exercise can take as long as you want, but in the context of this Bible study, 10 to 20 minutes should be sufficient.

The meditations that follow are provided only to help group participants use this prayer form, but note that *lectio* is intended to bring one to a place of prayerful contemplation where the Word of God speaks to the hearer from his or her heart. (See page 7 for further instruction.)

Jesus' testimony to John the Baptist (11:2–6)

Jesus points out that he has fulfilled the expectations of the prophets concerning the "one who is to come," namely, one who heals the afflicted, raises the dead, and preaches to the poor. Jesus' mission is not to condemn, but to bring salvation. This compassion and mercy of Jesus are so dominant in Jesus' life that they reveal the great love and concern God has for us.

✠ *What can I learn from this passage?*

The greatness of John the Baptist (11:7–19)

Within the Catholic Church, we have those who support particular devotions and others who practice a different form of spirituality. The manner in which we approach God and our attitudes toward God may differ in some way. However, we share a common faith that proclaims Jesus is the Christ, the Son of God, who brought us salvation through his passion, death, and resurrection, and we express this faith as a community in our liturgical worship.

✠ *What can I learn from this passage?*

The unrepentant towns (11:20–24)

Jesus warns the towns of the punishment in store for them because they witnessed his miracles and heard his words yet did not accept him. They overlooked the good deeds he had performed and refused to change their lives. In our lives, we have good and bad experiences. We easily accept the good gifts God gives us, but we can be tempted to blame God for our difficult times. Although God does allow evil to happen in the world, God does not plan it. God grieves with us over the pain in our lives.

✠ *What can I learn from this passage?*

Knowledge of God (11:25–30)

Once we recognize the love Jesus has for us and respond to that love, our need to follow his commands becomes easier for us. Reflection on Jesus' life and message helps us to understand and love him more, and following him becomes less difficult. When we reflect on our relationship with Jesus, we begin to "know" him, and knowing him is to love him and to willingly bear all, even death, for him. This is what Jesus meant when he said his yoke is easy and his burden light.

✠ *What can I learn from this passage?*

Jesus' disciples pluck grain on the Sabbath (12:1–8)

For Christians, the Lord's Day is dedicated mainly to worship as a community. Jesus regularly went to the synagogue on the Sabbath, giving us an example of how we should spend the Lord's Day. At the time of our baptism, the Church, the community of the body of Christ, welcomed us with great joy. As we share in the Eucharist, we reconfirm our baptismal vows by which we committed ourselves to worship with the community each Lord's Day. On the Lord's Day, we worship God the Father in, with, and through Jesus Christ in the unity of the Holy Spirit. Jesus is truly the Lord of the Sabbath and points out that the Sabbath is given for the good of human beings.

✠ *What can I learn from this passage?*

Jesus cures on the Sabbath (12:9–14)

On their way to Sunday worship one winter day, a man and his wife looked on in horror as the car in front of them skidded on the ice and crashed into a tree near the road. They rushed to the car to find a young man unconscious and slouched over the steering wheel. After spending the morning in the hospital with this stranger, they were able to leave when the man's relatives arrived and thanked them for their concern. Later, when they asked their pastor if they had displeased God by missing the Sunday liturgy, the pastor answered that God would have been more displeased if they had come to worship instead of staying and supporting the wounded man.

✠ *What can I learn from this passage?*

Jesus, the chosen servant (12:15–21)

When we sit at a table in a restaurant, a server will approach us and say, "Hello, my name is _____ and I will be your server today." Jesus gives us an example of being a servant in all that he did. Just as Jesus came as a servant, so we come in his place, chosen to take the place of a servant to the world. We can offer ourselves to Jesus as a servant each day with a morning prayer such as, "Good morning, Jesus, my name is _____, and I will be your servant today." Jesus, the servant, needs us to be his servants in the world.

✠ *What can I learn from this passage?*

Jesus and Beelzebul (12:22–37)

Many people who criticize goodness often expose their own weakness. Jealous people often accuse others of being jealous, gossiping people often accuse others of being gossips, and selfish people often accuse others of being selfish. Jesus provides a way of proving that a person is good or evil. Look at the results. Are people helped or hindered? Does one produce good fruit or bad? Jesus is telling the crowd to judge the Pharisees by using the accusations of the Pharisees against them. In this passage, they are far from producing good fruit.

✠ *What can I learn from this passage?*

The sign of Jonah (12:38–42)

God is with us in our daily life. The signs of God's presence are all around us, but we often overlook them. We pray for a safe trip and we travel safely. God's signs will always come in a concealed manner. Did God answer our prayer or would we have had a safe trip if we had not prayed? God may send signs, but they will always be hard to perceive. Jesus tells us that God is with us and loves us. That is the only sign we need.

✠ *What can I learn from this passage?*

The return of the evil spirit (12:43–45)

Sinners may confess their sins and leave the worship area with a feeling of relief that they are now free from sin, but that does not mean they are free from the temptation to commit that sin again. The Church stresses that a person must have a sincere desire not to commit a particular sin again, but we are weak and temptations are strong. Jesus reminds us that when we get rid of our demons, they are roaming around, looking for a way to get back into our lives.

✠ *What can I learn from this passage?*

Jesus' family and the will of God (12:46–50)

Our spiritual relationship with Christ makes high demands that many of us overlook. Belonging to the family of Jesus demands that we follow the dedication and example of Jesus. In Saint Paul's Letter to the Romans, we read, "The Spirit itself bears witness with our spirit that we are children of God, and if children, then heirs, heirs of God and joint heirs with Christ, if only we suffer with him so that we may also be glorified with him" (8:16–17). This is the major challenge of belonging to Jesus' family.

✠ *What can I learn from this passage?*

PART 2: INDIVIDUAL STUDY (MATTHEW 13:1–53)

Jesus continues to teach the crowds, but he does so in parables that he must explain to his disciples, while those who reject him do not have the ability to grasp the meaning of the parables.

Day 1: The Parable of the Sower (13:1–23)

Although the leaders of the people reject Jesus, the crowds still follow him. In this episode they become so numerous that Jesus has to sit in a boat while the people stand along the lake shore. This short introduction serves as a transition from the narrative section to the discourse section of this book.

Matthew closely follows Mark (4:1–20) in his presentation of the story of the sower who goes out to sow the seed. Jesus first tells the story with no explanation. The sower threw the seed upon the footpath, on the rocky ground, and among thorns. In all three cases, the seed did not produce fruit. The seed that fell upon good ground not only produced a harvest, but it produced an amazing harvest of a hundred, sixty, or thirtyfold.

When the disciples ask Jesus why he speaks in parables, he answers that he speaks this way for those who are open to his message, while those who have closed their ears to his message will not understand him. Mark gives a different reason. In his gospel, Jesus takes his disciples away from the crowd to explain the parable to them, and he tells them that he teaches in the form of parables so that the people who do not accept him may not understand what he is teaching. Matthew blames the hearers for not understanding. He continues to quote from the Old Testament and gives the reason for teaching in parables as a fulfillment of the prophecy of Isaiah (6:9–10), who states that the people can listen, but they will not understand because they have closed their eyes and ears (of faith) to the message of Jesus. Those who listen to Jesus' message with faith are called "blessed." They have the privilege of sharing in a gift sought by the prophets and saints of the past.

After this dialogue with his disciples, Jesus explains the parable. It is not clear whether Matthew includes the crowd, although it seems Jesus is speaking only to the disciples. The explanation of the parable makes the message an allegory rather than a parable. A parable has a single point, whereas an allegory has a point for each part of the story. The seed that fell upon the footpath, the rocky ground, and among thorns is the Word of God that does not find a firm foundation and is lost. The seed that falls upon good ground is the Word of God that is received and accepted and bears a yield of a hundred or sixty or thirtyfold for the kingdom of heaven.

Lectio Divina

Spend 8 to 10 minutes in silent contemplation of the following passage:

> Saint Augustine was born in 354. The seed of Christianity was sown in his heart early in life, but his worldly desires soon smothered it, and he led a life of loose morals for a long period of time, taking a mistress and eventually fathering a child. After struggling with several approaches to understanding where his life was taking him, he broke down in tears, and in the midst of his sobs, he heard a child singing over and over again, "Take and read. Take and read." He had the Bible with him, so he opened it and found where it was written, "not in orgies and drunkenness, not in promiscuity and licentiousness, not in rivalry and jealousy. But put on the Lord Jesus Christ, and make no provision for the desires of the flesh" (Romans 13:13–14). In that instant, Augustine began his journey to becoming a great theologian and a great saint. At one time in his life the seed fell among thorns, but in the end, it fell on good soil and produced a hundredfold.

> ✠ *What can I learn from this passage?*

Day 2: The Parable of the Weeds and the Wheat (13:24–43)

Jesus tells a parable about a man who sowed good seed in his field, only to find that an enemy had sown weeds among the wheat during the night. When the servants ask if they should root out the weeds, the owner decides to wait until the harvest to avoid the wheat's being rooted out as well. Matthew continues with the theme of separation at the time of Judgment by stating that the weeds will be separated from the wheat at the harvest time; the weeds will then be burned and the wheat stored.

Jesus begins this and other stories of the kingdom with the words, "The kingdom of heaven may be likened to…." Matthew is telling us that the kingdom of heaven is like the whole event recounted here and not like any particular part of the story.

The disciples will ask Jesus to explain the story of the weeds and wheat, but not before Matthew sandwiches in two more parables. In these parables Jesus speaks of the small beginnings of the kingdom. A tiny mustard seed eventually becomes a great tree, and yeast makes dough rise. The amount of flour used is ridiculously large, a fact intended by Jesus to show the enormous growth of the kingdom and to show that the reign of God will not be limited to a small area but will reach out to the world. Matthew continues to portray Jesus as the fulfillment of the Old Testament expectation by stating that the expected one was destined to speak in parables. (See Psalm 78:2.)

When the disciples ask Jesus to explain the story of the weeds and the wheat, Jesus explains it in such a way that it becomes an allegory rather than a parable. As with the other parables that have developed this way, this could be the result of the preaching of the early Church, which saw meaning in every detail of the story. The farmer is Jesus, the field is the world, the good seed are the members of the Church, the weeds are the evil people, and the enemy is the devil. The story becomes one of Final Judgment. The angels (the harvesters) will collect all those who are evil and throw them into the everlasting fire, while the good will share in God's kingdom. Matthew could be addressing the early Church members as he calls all people to heed what they hear; within the membership of the early Church, one may find weeds alongside the wheat.

Lectio Divina

Spend 8 to 10 minutes in silent contemplation of the following passage:

> Many people wish to remain close to Christ, but they are so weak they keep falling into sin. Many eventually reach the stage later in life where they are able to overcome their weakness and remain faithful to God. Early in life they looked like the weeds, but God gave them time to prove that they are indeed the wheat. We cannot judge who are the weeds and who is the wheat.

✠ *What can I learn from this passage?*

Day 3: Parables of the Treasure, the Pearl, and the Net (13:44–53)

Jesus tells his listeners that the kingdom of heaven is like a buried treasure or a fine pearl. People sell everything they have for these precious gifts. In the same way, people should invest everything they have in seeking the kingdom of heaven.

The parable of the net reminded the early Church that not everyone who belongs to the kingdom will reach its fulfillment. On the Day of Judgment, the angels of the Lord will separate the evil ones from the righteous, and they will hurl the evil ones into a place of eternal fire. Some who are evil will belong to the kingdom of heaven here on Earth, but on the Day of Judgment they will be rejected for their sinful actions.

Matthew places greater emphasis on the understanding of the disciples than Mark does. Matthew strives to present them in as favorable a light as possible. They claim to understand what Jesus has told them. From the mouth of Jesus, Matthew gives a short lesson to the Christian scribes of the day. They must interpret the Old Testament in light of the person and message of Jesus Christ. They have a privileged position, like the head of a household, and are to draw out of the treasure of the Old Testament a deeper understanding of the New Age. The author of Matthew's Gospel provides a perfect example of the Christian scribe in the early Church.

Lectio Divina

Spend 8 to 10 minutes in silent contemplation of the following passage:

God has blessed us with Christian scribes like the author of the Gospel of Matthew who can draw images from the Old Testament and show us how they apply to Jesus. The reign of God becomes clearer to us as we read the gospels and learn about Jesus and his message. Reading the Scriptures is important for our understanding of the reign of God, and they instruct us on how to remain faithful to God's reign.

✠ *What can I learn from this passage?*

Review Questions

1. What is the message of the parable of the sower who went out to sow his seed?

2. What is the message of the parable of the weeds and the wheat growing together?

3. How do the parables of the mustard seed and the leaven in bread apply to Jesus' message of the kingdom of heaven?

4. What do the parables of the treasure in the field and the fine pearl tell us about the kingdom of heaven?

5. What warning do we find in the parable of the net and the catch of fish?

The Mystery Fully Revealed

MATTHEW 13:54–16

After they got into the boat, the wind died down. Those who were in the boat did him homage, saying, "Truly, you are the Son of God" (14:32–33).

Opening Prayer (SEE PAGE 14)

Context

Part 1: Matthew 13:54—15:31 The author introduces this book, which speaks of the kingdom of heaven and the Church. The people of Jesus' hometown and Herod, who has John the Baptist put to death, lack faith in Jesus. Jesus feeds five thousand in the desert and walks on water, both signs of Jesus' divine powers. When he encounters a woman who is not a Jew, Jesus performs a miracle for her because of her great faith, and he continues to heal a large number of people.

Part 2: Matthew 15:32—16 Jesus feeds four thousand people in Gentile territory, and he later warns his disciples not to be influenced by the Pharisees. Jesus becomes more clearly identified as Peter declares that he is the "Messiah, the Son of the living God," but Peter soon shows that he does not know the full import of what he's saying when he denies that Jesus will suffer, die, and be raised. Jesus uses the occasion to explain the challenges of discipleship.

PART 1: GROUP STUDY (MATTHEW 13:54—15:31)

Read aloud Matthew 13:54—15:31

13:54–58 Jesus' rejection at Nazareth

Matthew continues to follow Mark closely in his narrative, although he effectively shortens many of the narratives to present an image of Jesus who is more in control of the events surrounding his message. Jesus returns to his "native place," which is known from the Gospel of Mark and the infancy narratives to be Nazareth. Matthew mentions that Jesus speaks in "their" synagogue instead of in "the" synagogue. During the time of Matthew, Christians were not allowed to take part in the synagogue service. Matthew could be reflecting the thinking of his own day in speaking of "their" synagogue. Matthew continues to show special respect for Jesus. In the Gospel of Mark (6:3), the townspeople identify Jesus as the "carpenter," but Matthew has them identify him as the "carpenter's son." In this way, Matthew avoids identifying Jesus with any worldly trade. The townspeople further identify Jesus through his family. The brothers and sisters of Jesus may refer to relatives other than immediate brothers and sisters. During the time of Jesus, people referred to cousins as brothers and sisters.

Because the townspeople believed they knew Jesus so well, they refused to accept that he was different from them. Their amazement turns to scorn and they refuse to hear his message. Matthew tells us that Jesus did not perform any miracles there because of the people's lack of faith, implying that he could have performed miracles but decided not to do so. Mark states in his gospel (6:5) that Jesus could not perform any miracles there because of their lack of faith.

14:1–12 The death of John the Baptist

John the Baptist prepared the way of the Lord not only by preaching about Jesus but also by pointing out the path that Jesus would follow in living out his ministry. Matthew follows Mark's Gospel closely, but he shortens Mark's narrative (6:17–29) and underlines more forcefully the relationship between John and Jesus. Just as Herod wants to kill John but is afraid of the people's reaction, so the leaders of the people will hesitate to kill Jesus for the same reason. A Roman ruler puts John to death, and Roman rule will put Jesus to death. After the death of John, his disciples come to bury his body. After the death of Jesus, his disciples will bury his body. Herod fears that Jesus is John raised from the dead; Jesus will indeed be raised from the dead. As in Mark, Herodias, erroneously identified as the wife of Herod's brother Philip, persuades her daughter to ask for the head of John the Baptist. Herodias was actually the wife of Herod's half-brother, who also had the name Herod. John had accused Herod of wrongdoing in taking Herodias as his wife. Matthew links the story with Jesus by having Herod wonder about Jesus at the beginning of the narrative and having Jesus receive word of John's death at the end.

14:13–21 Feeding the five thousand

News of the death of John the Baptist becomes the occasion for Jesus' departure into the desert. Unlike the Gospel of Mark (6:34–44), which states that Jesus taught a crowd at this time, Matthew presents Jesus compassionately healing the sick. This compassion extends to the need to feed the people in the desert. When the disciples urge Jesus to send the people away so they might buy food to eat, Jesus tells the disciples to feed the people. The mission of the disciples will be to share the gifts of Jesus with all people. The disciples, who are presented in a more favorable light in the Gospel of Matthew, do not debate with Jesus as they do in the Gospel of Mark. They tell Jesus that they have five loaves and a couple of fish, and they follow Jesus' directions.

The manner in which Jesus blesses the bread echoes the Last Supper and the eucharistic celebration in the early Church. Jesus gives the bread to his disciples to distribute. Just as the gifts of Jesus will be given in abundance through the Church, so an abundance of bread is given, and twelve baskets are left over. The number twelve points to the Church, which is the new Israel led by the twelve apostles.

14:22–36 Jesus walks on water

Although Matthew continues to draw on Mark (6:45–52) for his message, he adds details that give more significance to Jesus' walking on water. In the Gospel of Matthew, the storm has many of the aspects of an apocalyptic event.

As the disciples struggle against strong headwinds, they see Jesus walking on the water and fear he is a ghost. Matthew adds the details about Peter's request to come across the water to Jesus. Jesus shows his power over the elements of nature by walking on the water, and he shows he can share this power with others such as Peter. The people of Jesus' day believed the sea symbolized chaos and evil. Jesus' power over the sea is presented not only as divine power over the elements but also as power over evil in the world.

Peter comes walking to Jesus on the water. Like later in his life, as long as he keeps his eyes on Jesus, he is able to do great and wonderful deeds. Once he looks away from Jesus to the surrounding storm, he begins to sink. A quick prayer, "Lord, save me!" is enough for Jesus to reach out and lift Peter up. The scene previews a future time when Peter will speak bravely of following Jesus to death, only to deny him when the "storm" becomes intense. Peter will ask for and receive forgiveness from Jesus for his failings. In the Gospel of Mark, the disciples are confused about Jesus, but Matthew portrays them as paying homage to Jesus and proclaiming him as the Son of God.

Matthew also shares a special message with his readers through this story. The early Church is like a boat struggling against the storms of persecution and the power of evil. Peter has an important role in the early Church and is held in high esteem by the time Matthew writes his gospel. Some of the members of the early Church, caught in the confusion of the evil around them, are faltering in their faith. Through this story, they are reminded to call to Jesus to save them.

Unlike the rejection Jesus faced in his native place of Nazareth, he now encounters crowds who spread word of his arrival and who come seeking a cure by simply touching a fringe of his cloak. Because of their simple faith, those who touch the garment are healed.

15:1–20 Tradition of the elders

According to the section on the Law for priests in the Book of Leviticus, a priest must first perform certain ritual cleansings before eating (22:4–7). The Pharisees, who did not belong to the priestly cast, applied this law to all the people of Israel because they believed the Israelites were truly the priestly people of God. When the Pharisees question Jesus about his disciples' disregard for the Law by not washing their hands before eating, Jesus challenges them. The people of Jesus' day accepted the role of the Pharisees in interpreting the Law, but Jesus accuses them of actually changing the Law. As an example, he challenges their change of the law that obliges people to care for their parents. According to the Pharisees, those who dedicate their goods to God are exempt from the law of caring for their parents. Jesus accuses the Pharisees of doing away with a law of God. Jesus labels the Pharisees as hypocrites, those about whom Isaiah spoke when he said, "This people draws near with words only and honors me with their lips alone, though their hearts are far from me, and fear of me has become mere precept of human teaching" (29:13).

Jesus calls the crowd together and challenges the very roots of Jewish belief about the eating of unclean foods. Within the early Church, a controversy arose concerning the dietary laws carried over from Judaism. The missionaries to the Gentiles struggled to rid Christianity of these dietary laws because they were such a burden to the new converts. The converts from Judaism struggled to keep them as part of Christianity. By Matthew's time, the dietary laws were no longer in effect for Christians, but some still tried to enforce them. Not only does Matthew have Jesus speaking to the people of Jesus' day concerning the dietary laws, but he also has him speaking to the people of the early Church. Jesus proclaims that true uncleanliness consists in the words and deeds of a person. In the early Church, a council held at Jerusalem dealt with the problem of these dietary laws, and the Church leaders at the time agreed that these laws should not be imposed upon the new converts from among the Gentiles.

When Jesus' disciples tell him that the Pharisees were scandalized by his words, Jesus completely rejects these leaders. They are not planted by God, so they will be uprooted. False interpreters of the Law are like blind guides who can only lead others who are blind. Those who can see never follow blind guides. The pit toward which they are heading is an image of harsh judgment. Not only does Matthew use this passage to show Jesus' break with the Pharisees, but he also uses it for the readers of his own day who have broken with the Pharisees and who no longer accept them as the interpreters of the Law. Jesus gives a new lesson to his followers. He explains to Peter that those things that enter a person pass out in the ways established by nature. What people speak comes from their mind and heart, and this is what makes a person unclean. Jesus gives a list of these things. This list of evil deeds was apparently one of several lists of sin used in the preaching in the early Church. Matthew puts this list on the lips of Jesus. Lest anyone miss the message, Matthew has Jesus repeat the fact that eating with unwashed hands does not make a person unclean.

15:21–31 Healing the Canaanite woman and other healings

The land of Tyre and Sidon is situated in present-day Lebanon. A Canaanite woman, a non-Jew, calls out to Jesus with words that express her faith. She calls Jesus by the titles "Lord" and "Son of David." She begs him to cast a demon out of her daughter. When the disciples ask Jesus to get rid of her, Jesus seems intent on ignoring her. Matthew makes clear that Jesus saw his mission as directed toward the people of Israel. The message of this story and the entire gospel centers on how Christianity was to spread to the believing Gentiles after the resurrection of Jesus.

When the woman pays homage to Jesus, he replies with an apparent lack of compassion, saying it is not right to give to dogs what belongs to sons and daughters. The Jews referred to the Gentile pagans by the derogatory title of "dogs"; the sons and daughters are the people of Israel. The woman, standing firm in her request, accepts the insult and states that even dogs eat that which falls from the table. The encounter is presented in the form of a strong debate often used among the rabbis of the day. The faith of the woman gains Jesus' approval and he grants her wish. The woman becomes, for Matthew, an image of the Gentiles who come to believe in Jesus. Although they did not have a direct right to the promises of the Chosen People, their persistent faith led Jesus to accept them.

As Jesus begins his acts of healing in this passage, he takes the position of authority as he did in the Sermon on the Mount. He goes up the mountainside and sits down. The miracles summarized in this section (curing those who are lame, deformed, blind, mute, and others) recall the prophecies of Isaiah (29:18, 35:5–6), who speaks of the servant who is to come. The authority of Jesus becomes evident not through his words, but through his actions. This short passage serves as a transition to the feeding of the four thousand in the desert.

Review Questions

1. How does the death of John the Baptist foreshadow that of Jesus?
2. What is significant about Jesus' feeding five thousand in the desert?
3. What messages do we find in the story of Jesus' and Peter's walking on water?
4. What do we learn from Jesus' confrontation with the Canaanite woman?

Closing Prayer (SEE PAGE 14)

Pray the closing prayer now or after *lectio divina*.

Lectio Divina (SEE PAGE 7)

Relax your body and maintain a posture of prayer (back straight, eyes shut, feet flat on the floor). This exercise can take as long as you want, but in the context of this Bible study, 10 to 20 minutes should be sufficient.

The meditations that follow are provided only to help group participants use this prayer form, but note that *lectio* is intended to bring one to a place of prayerful contemplation where the Word of God speaks to the hearer from his or her heart. (See page 7 for further instruction.)

Jesus' rejection at Nazareth (13:54–58)

Jesus grew up in Nazareth, and his neighbors took it for granted that he was no different than they were. Because of their rejection of Jesus, they missed the presence of the Son of God in their midst. In the same manner, we could miss the presence of Jesus in our midst in the Eucharist when we take it for granted. The effect of the Eucharist in our life depends on the extent of our faith in celebrating the sacrament.

✠ *What can I learn from this passage?*

The death of John the Baptist (14:1–12)

In many ways, Jesus' passion and death become a prelude to the life of Jesus' followers who would find themselves suffering and dying for Christ. When we realize that Jesus and his followers seek the good of the poor and oppressed, preaching a message of peace rather than violence, it is surprising that so many people throughout the world put so much energy into killing Christians. Very often, those who kill them are driven by fear and ignorance.

✠ *What can I learn from this passage?*

Feeding the five thousand (14:13–21)

As we share in the Eucharist, we are sharing in the Last Supper that Jesus longed to share with his disciples. Jesus is still sharing with us each time we celebrate the Eucharist, giving us strength for our journey, just as he gave food to the people in the desert to help sustain them for their journey. No matter how difficult our lives may become, we still have a compassionate Jesus as a companion for our journey, and we continually renew our friendship with the loving and compassionate Christ in the celebration of the Eucharist.

✠ *What can I learn from this passage?*

Jesus walks on water (14:22–36)

When we celebrate a sacrament, we have our eye on Christ and bravely declare that we can live up to the commitments involved in living that sacrament. We are walking on water. But when we live our everyday lives, we become surrounded by the storms and may take our eyes off Christ and begin to sink. But we have moments of reflection to recall Jesus' presence in our life. We begin to walk on the water again as we focus on Christ.

✠ *What can I learn from this passage?*

Tradition of the elders (15:1–20)

The reading about the unclean food shows that conflict existed even in the early Church. Conflict often shows itself in our own time when changes are made in the celebration of our eucharistic liturgy. In our era we can expect differences of opinion, but when we begin to worship, we set aside our differences and worship as a loving community praising God. In the end, worshiping God in accordance with the liturgical guidelines is what's important.

✠ *What can I learn from this passage?*

Healing the Canaanite woman and other healings (15:21–31)

The Gentile woman who wanted a miracle from Jesus shows her strong and persistent faith as she debates with Jesus. Jesus seems to enjoy the debate, testing her faith to see if she would give up. When she persisted, Jesus praises her for her faith and heals her daughter. The passage teaches that we should never give up when we pray. We must pray with persistence and faith. If God wishes to answer our prayer in a different manner, we will recognize it.

✠ *What can I learn from this passage?*

PART 2: INDIVIDUAL STUDY (MATTHEW 15:32—16)

Jesus reaches out to all people, Jew as well as Gentile. Those who are open to his gifts are able to receive them, while those opposed to Jesus cannot recognize the gifts he has to offer. Peter receives the gift of identifying Christ, but like the rest of us, he must struggle to understand the deep message of Jesus' life and message.

Day 1: Feeding the Four Thousand (15:32–39)

The feeding of the four thousand in the desert follows the story in Mark's Gospel and strongly resembles the feeding of the five thousand in Matthew's Gospel. It is probably the same story told with slight variations for the Gentile audience. The miracle takes place in Gentile territory, and the motive for the miracle is Jesus' compassion for the crowd who have been three days without eating. The number seven is very significant to the Gentile audience, who saw that number as a sign of perfection. Instead of five loaves, the disciples have seven, and instead of twelve baskets, the disciples gather up seven baskets of food after all have been fed. The number twelve would not have had the same significance for a Gentile audience as it did for a Jewish audience. The manner in which Jesus blesses the loaves again reflects the eucharistic meal. Jesus dismisses the crowd and leaves that territory.

Lectio Divina

Spend 8 to 10 minutes in silent contemplation of the following passage:

Jesus came for all people, Jews as well as Gentiles, men as well as women, slaves as well as free, sinners as well as saints. Wherever we fit, we can say that Jesus came for us, and Jesus shared the eucharistic meal with all people of whatever race or nationality. In this passage, as well as the passage in which he feeds the five thousand, we find that Jesus takes pity on the crowd. Jesus seems able to experience their pain and does something about it. His disciples are called to do the same.

✠ *What can I learn from this passage?*

Day 2: The Demand for a Sign (16:1–4)

The Pharisees and the Sadducees join forces to confront Jesus by asking for a sign from heaven. Jesus rebukes them for their inability to read the signs of the times in relation to the Messiah. They are able to read the signs of nature, but not the signs of God. This rebuke must have stung the Pharisees, because they considered themselves the interpreters of the Law and the ones who were supposed to understand the message of God for Israel. Although Jesus mentions the sign of Jonah as the only sign they will receive, he does not explicitly connect it to his death and resurrection as he has done in the past.

Lectio Divina

Spend 8 to 10 minutes in silent contemplation of the following passage:

> A good practice for all of us at the end of each day would be to examine that day's signs of God's love. When tragedies occur, we blame God, but our life is filled with a number of signs of God's goodness. Unlike the Sadducees and Pharisees in this passage, we can read the signs of God's love for us if we reflect on our events.

✠ *What can I learn from this passage?*

Day 3: The Leaven of the Pharisees and Sadducees (16:5–12)

When Jesus warns his disciples against the leaven of the Pharisees and the Sadducees, they think he is alluding to the fact that they brought no bread with them. In the Gospel of Mark (8:15), Jesus links the Pharisees with the followers of Herod, but Matthew speaks instead of the Pharisees and the Sadducees. Matthew is concerned with false witnesses within Judaism, and this could account for his mentioning the Sadducees instead of the Herodians.

Jesus rebukes his disciples for not understanding his message, and he asks pointed questions concerning his previous miracles of twice multiplying the loaves and fish. Recalling these miracles should have helped them realize that Jesus could provide bread if he wished. They should have realized that he was not speaking about food, but about the influence of the Pharisees and Sadducees, which can inflate the minds of many people just as leaven makes the dough rise. Matthew, with his continued respect for the disciples, portrays them as finally understanding Jesus' explanation. In the Gospel of Mark, they still do not understand.

Lectio Divina

Spend 8 to 10 minutes in silent contemplation of the following passage:

> In our own day, our leaders are not necessarily religious leaders, but government leaders who touch the religious and social life of all of us. When governments abandon the rights of some in our society to obtain life, liberty, and the pursuit of happiness, people have a right to speak out for justice for all. Respect for authority can challenge leaders to remain within the boundaries of the Law of God. This is an act of virtue, and it leaves no room for violence but only for using peaceful means to obtain the rights to life, liberty, and the pursuit of happiness, which is what our country espouses.

✠ *What can I learn from this passage?*

Day 4: Peter Professes Jesus as the Christ (16:13–20)

The seat of Caesarea Philippi is situated in northern Palestine. Jesus asks his disciples, "Who do people say the Son of Man is?" In the Gospel of Mark (8:27), Jesus asks, "Who do people say that I am?" The title Son of Man aligns Jesus with his messianic title, thus pointing to a spiritual rather than an earthly kingdom. It could also pertain to Jesus as a human being. Who do people say this human being named Jesus is?

The disciples respond that some see him as John the Baptist returned from the dead, as Herod did earlier, while others see him as Elijah (who was expected to return before Judgment Day), Jeremiah (a great prophet whose name is not mentioned in the Gospel of Mark), or one of the prophets. In the Book of Deuteronomy, Moses spoke of a great prophet who is to come: "A prophet like me will the LORD, your God, raise up for you from among your own kindred; that is the one to whom you shall listen" (18:15).

When Jesus directly asks his disciples who they believe he is, Peter speaks on their behalf and proclaims Jesus as "the Messiah, the Son of the living God." Up to this point, Matthew has closely followed the story as found in the Gospel of Mark. With the addition of the phrase "the Son of the living God," Matthew presents a developed theology not found in Mark. The community for which Matthew is writing had come to a deeper understanding of the mystery of Jesus, and Matthew places this development on the lips of Peter. Jesus tells Peter he has not gained this understanding on his own but that it is a gift from God.

When Jesus first speaks to Peter, he addresses him as "Simon, son of Jonah," but then he changes his name to "Peter," which means "rock." Jesus states that he will build his Church upon this rock. As a true witness to Christ and his resurrection, Peter will be the foundation of the Church. No power of evil or death will be able to overcome the Church. Jesus, in speaking of the Church, is speaking of a community of believers. Jesus gives Peter the keys to the kingdom, along with the power of binding and loosing. This recalls the words of Isaiah (22:22), who spoke of a new ruler of Judea who would be given the key to the House of David and would have the power to open and shut access whenever he wished. The power of binding and loosing refers to the power of interpreting the Law, as well as the power to cut people off from the community. The key is the symbol of authority Peter receives from Jesus.

The addition of Peter proclaiming that Jesus is the "Son of the living God," as well as the granting of authority to Peter by Jesus, are most likely later additions developed within the early Church and widely accepted by the community for which Matthew wrote his gospel. Matthew returns to Mark as his source and records that Jesus ordered his disciples not to spread the news that he was the Messiah. The implication is that no one would understand the true meaning of the term *messiah*.

Lectio Divina

Spend 8 to 10 minutes in silent contemplation of the following passage:

Our faith does not come because we are more brilliant than others who lack faith. It comes as a gift, an inspiration from God, as it did for Peter. If we can say with Peter that Jesus is the Christ, the Son of God, and truly believe what we say, we do so by the grace of God. When we profess faith that Jesus is the Christ, the Son of the living God, we have to bring that faith into our daily lives. Somehow we must reflect the presence of Christ in the world.

✠ *What can I learn from this passage?*

Day 5: Jesus Predicts His Death and Resurrection (16:21–23)

Peter's profession of faith signals a change in the Gospel of Matthew, as it does in the other synoptic gospels. Up to this point, the core of Jesus' message was the coming of the kingdom. Jesus now begins to speak more often of his passion, death, and resurrection. In the first of three predictions, he tells how he must go to Jerusalem, where he will suffer at the hands of religious leaders, die, and be raised on the third day. Matthew shows that Jesus is following a certain destiny when he states that he "must go to Jerusalem." Peter rejects Jesus' words and now becomes the tempter. Jesus responds harshly to Peter, rebuking him in the same way he rebuked Satan during the temptations in the desert, ordering Peter to get behind him, out of his sight. (See 4:10.) This is as harsh as a slap to Peter's face. In the temptations in the desert, Satan tries to lure Jesus into a life of luxury and painlessness, which Satan realizes is contrary to Jesus' mission. Peter is speaking like Satan, seeking a comfortable life for Jesus. Jesus accuses Peter of not thinking as God thinks, but as human beings think. Jesus has an eternal view of his life. It is not a life lived for himself and his own glory, but a life lived to bring salvation to the world.

Lectio Divina

Spend 8 to 10 minutes in silent contemplation of the following passage:

Jesus never mentions his passion and death without also speaking of his resurrection. Peter hears only the words about Jesus' passion and death, and he cannot accept such a horrible thought. Peter has received his proclamation of faith through the inspiration of God, but he must now understand what it means. Although we live thousands of years after the resurrection of Christ and believe that Jesus is the Christ, the Son of God, we must still struggle to understand the depth of this mystery. We are continually learning.

✠ *What can I learn from this passage?*

Day 6: The Conditions of Discipleship (16:24–28)

Once Jesus establishes that he must undergo his passion, death, and resurrection, his followers must be prepared to do the same. To deny oneself in this life for the sake of the kingdom leads to eternal life, while the desire to preserve oneself in this life will lead to a loss of eternal life. We gain nothing if we gain the whole world and lose eternal life in the process. One of the temptations Jesus faced when Satan visited him in the desert was to preserve his life. If Jesus would pay homage to Satan, then Satan would give him all the kingdoms of the world.

Jesus speaks of the "Son of Man" who will come in glory, accompanied by his angels. This apocalyptic image of the Son of Man reflects the belief of the early Church, which looked expectantly to the imminent Second Coming of Christ and the Day of Judgment. Because the people of Matthew's day believed the Second Coming would happen soon, they expected some would still be alive when it did happen.

Lectio Divina

Spend 8 to 10 minutes in silent contemplation of the following passage:

Jesus tells us we must be ready to pick up our cross and follow him. The cross is not always painful, but it can often demand a difficult manner of life. It means remaining faithful to our commitments, commitments that can become challenging in time. Paul the Apostle says it well when he writes, "None of us lives for oneself, and no one dies for oneself. For if we live, we live for the Lord, and if we die, we die for the Lord" (Romans 14:7–8).

✠ *What can I learn from this passage?*

Review Questions

1. Why does Jesus feel a need to confront the Pharisees concerning their interpretation of the Law?

2. What significant message do we receive from Peter's profession of faith and his later rejection of Jesus' prediction of his passion, death, and resurrection?

3. Why is it important that Jesus' disciples be willing to suffer and die?

Jesus Moves From Galilee to Judea

MATTHEW 17—20

Whoever wishes to be great among you shall be your servant; whoever wishes to be first among you shall be your slave (20:26–27).

Opening Prayer (SEE PAGE 14)

Context

Part 1: Matthew 17—18 Three of Jesus' disciples witness his transfiguration, but they still do not understand his identity. Jesus continues to heal, predict his passion, teach about humility in the kingdom of heaven, and explain God's great joy over sinners who repent and the call to forgive others as God forgives us.

Part 2: Matthew 19—20 Jesus supports God's plan of marriage in creation, blesses children, and teaches the difficulty of entering the kingdom of heaven with great wealth. He reminds his disciples that the ways of God are not the ways of human beings as he tells about a landowner who gave a full day's salary to all his workers, from those who worked the least hours to those who worked all day. After predicting his passion, death, and resurrection, he must still remind his disciples of their call to serve in the kingdom of heaven. Jesus then heals two blind men as a sign that the disciples are still living with spiritual blindness.

PART 1: GROUP STUDY (MATTHEW 17—18)

Read aloud Matthew 17—18

17:1–8 The transfiguration of Jesus

The story of the transfiguration described in the Gospel of Matthew closely parallels the same story found in the Gospel of Mark (9:2–8). Most commentators believe the story developed within the preaching of the early Church and was eventually placed within the historical context of Jesus' ministry. The story has all the Old Testament elements of a heavenly visitation from God. The fact that Jesus takes Peter, James, and John up the mountain for this event underlines its importance. These same three disciples will share in the intimate scene of Jesus' agony in the garden.

Jesus appears in glory, conversing with Moses, who symbolizes the old Law, and Elijah, who symbolizes the prophets of the Old Testament. This scene illustrates that Jesus is the fulfillment of the Old Testament Law and the prophets. The cloud, which represents the presence of God, overshadows them as it does when God comes to the people of Israel in the desert. A voice from heaven proclaims the same message heard at the baptism of Jesus: "This is my beloved Son." Matthew adds that the disciples fall to the ground in the typical fashion of people filled with fear and reverence in the presence of God. Peter, always quick to speak, wishes to build three dwellings, just as the Israelites set up a tent for the glory of God in the desert. (See Exodus 33:7.) The scene ends quietly with Jesus urging his disciples to arise and have no fear.

17:9–13 The coming of Elijah

As Jesus and the disciples come down the mountain, Jesus orders them not to tell anyone about the vision until "after the Son of Man has been raised from the dead." Matthew, to avoid any sign of weakness on the part of the disciples, omits Mark's description of their inability to understand the words of Jesus. When the disciples ask when Elijah will come, Jesus states that Elijah has already come and the people did not recognize him. Jesus is alluding to John the Baptist, although he does not name him. When Jesus speaks of the suffering of Elijah and that he himself will suffer in the same manner, the disciples recognize that Jesus is speaking about John the Baptist. John foreshadows the suffering and death of Jesus.

17:14–23 Jesus heals a possessed boy

When Jesus comes down the mountain, a man with a son who has epilepsy begs Jesus to cast the demon out of the boy because Jesus' disciples could not do it. Matthew follows Mark's Gospel (9:14–29) closely in this story, although he shortens it and emphasizes the lack of faith of the disciples and the absence of faith in the present generation. After Jesus cures the boy, Matthew adds a private scene between Jesus and his disciples. Jesus tells the disciples that it was their lack of faith that hindered them from performing this miracle. Using the image of a tiny mustard seed, Jesus tells them that faith as small as that seed would be enough to perform great deeds. The image of moving mountains should not be taken literally. Jesus is telling his disciples that they can perform spiritual deeds as astounding as moving mountains if they have faith even as small as a mustard seed.

The second prediction of the passion, death, and resurrection of Jesus lacks many of the details of Jesus' earlier predictions. The fact that Jesus will be delivered into the hands of the enemy shows that God will allow this to happen. Unlike the Gospel of Mark (9:30–32), which speaks of the disciples as not understanding Jesus, Matthew portrays them as understanding and grieving at the news.

17:24–27 Paying the temple tax

Collectors of the temple tax ask Peter whether Jesus pays the tax, and Peter assures them that he does. The fact that the tax collectors approach Peter shows his position as the recognized leader of the Twelve. The story is meant to give a message to the early Church community, and it could actually have developed within the time of the early Church. According to Jewish Law, all Jews had to pay the temple tax, and Jesus would most likely have obeyed. At the time Matthew wrote his gospel, however, the temple tax was used for the upkeep of pagan temples, and the members of the early Church struggled with the fact that they were supporting a pagan cult.

Jesus asks Peter if the sons of a ruler must pay the tax or if the rule applies to foreigners alone. Peter answers that foreigners must pay the tax. Because Jesus is truly the Son of God, he should be exempt from the tax, but Jesus gives an example to his followers and pays the tax. Matthew protects the image of Jesus and Peter with the story of the fish from whose mouth the coin for the temple tax is taken. In this way, it does not come directly from Jesus or Peter.

18:1–5 The greatest in the reign of God

The fourth discourse begins as a reply to the disciples' question as to who is the greatest in the kingdom of heaven. Unlike Mark (9:33), who presents the disciples disputing who is the greatest, Matthew continues to protect the reputation of Jesus' disciples by having them sincerely ask Jesus this question. Jesus teaches the radical difference between the kingdom of heaven and the kingdom of the world. Jesus places a child in their midst and explains to them that those who become like little children will be the most important in the kingdom of heaven. Children did not receive the same tender response from people during the time of Jesus that they do today. They had no rights and no way of earning anything. All they had came as a gift. The disciples are directed to become as dependent as a little child to become important in the kingdom of heaven and to receive with love in the name of Jesus those who are as dependent as a little child.

18:6–14 Avoiding temptation

As Jesus speaks, he moves from the image of children to the image of the "little ones," a reference to the new disciples taking their first steps in the faith. The message is most likely addressed to the early Church, which was experiencing rapid growth in the number of converts from various backgrounds and cultures. Although stumbling blocks will arise, this does not excuse the one responsible for them.

The most feared form of death among the people of Jesus' day was death by drowning. The sea was the place of demons who were living in the pit of darkness. The wrath of God would be so great against those who erect stumbling blocks in the path of these little ones that they would consider this fearful death of drowning to be a more desirable end. Jesus admits that sin will come into the world, but woe to that person from whom evil comes. A person should be ready to go so far as to cut off a hand or a foot rather than put up stumbling blocks. Matthew has already used this image in the Sermon on the Mount.

The rabbis of Jesus' day taught that people had their own angels who stood before the throne of God. Jesus warns the people to remember the angels of these little ones who stand in God's presence. He tells the parable of the lost sheep and compares the sheep to one of the little ones. They are so important that if one of them should stray, the Church should search for that person and rejoice upon his or her return, like a celebration over the return of a lost sheep. In God's great plan, not even one of these little ones should be lost.

18:15–20 Norms for correcting another

Not only does Jesus speak about rejoicing at the return of the lost sheep, but he also speaks about some norms for gaining the lost sheep back. The offended person should first privately approach the offender for the sake of reconciliation. If this fails, Jesus advises the offended person to follow the Old Testament norm of asking two or three witnesses to approach the person with him. (See Deuteronomy 19:15.) Finally, Jesus directs that the offender be brought before the Church. This is the second time Matthew uses the term *Church* in his gospel. If this also fails, then the offender shall be treated as an outcast. When Matthew speaks about bringing the offender to the Church, he is most likely speaking of the local community of his own era. To Jewish society in the time of Jesus, the pagan Gentile and the sinful tax collector were considered outcasts. This idea amounted to excommunication. Such excommunication could not take place within the Church until the development of specific structures that were not in place until after the resurrection of Jesus. Matthew has apparently added details to the original message of Jesus to give direction to the people of the early Church community.

Just as Jesus gave Peter the power to bind and loose in an earlier passage of this gospel (16:19), he now gives this same power to the Church. The authority of the Church has the same force as the authority of Jesus.

Matthew then chooses to use a saying of Jesus concerning prayer. Jesus stresses the power of community at prayer when he states that he is in the midst of them when two or three are gathered together in his name.

Whatever they seek will be granted by God in heaven. He is most likely speaking of a group praying together, but not the Church at worship.

18:21–35 Forgiveness

Peter acts as spokesperson for the disciples and the readers of the gospel when he asks how many times he must forgive a person. He most likely feels very generous when he suggests that seven times would be a good number. Jesus tells Peter he should forgive seventy-seven times, which is another way of telling him that he should always forgive and not count how many times he does so. Jesus' answer actually does away with any thought of retaliation toward anyone who hurts us.

Jesus presents a parable about the kingdom of heaven, saying that it is like a king who decided to settle accounts with his slave. The king orders a slave who owes him a huge amount to be sold along with his wife, children, and property to pay the debt. The man pays homage to the king, promising to pay back in time the entire debt. The king has compassion on the slave and forgives him his debt. When that man leaves the presence of the king, he encounters a fellow servant who owes him a much smaller amount, and he casts the fellow servant into jail until he pays all. When the master hears what the forgiven slave has done, he hands him over to be tortured until he pays back all he owed.

This message pertains to the forgiveness of God. Because God has forgiven us a great debt, we should be willing to forgive others their debts, even if we must do so seventy-seven times. It does not matter how much we forgive; we will never equal the forgiveness God has shown to us. In this story of the Judgment Day, Jesus shows us the great mercy of God and calls us to practice mercy in our turn. Mercy is one of the central themes of the Gospel of Matthew. Jesus gives a dire warning that the one who is unmerciful will receive a deserved punishment for sins.

Review Questions

1. What is the message behind Jesus' transfiguration?
2. What did Jesus give as a reason for the disciples' inability to heal the boy with a demon?
3. What was Jesus' message about paying the temple tax?
4. Who is the greatest in the reign of God?
5. What does the parable of the lost sheep tell us about God's love for us?

Closing Prayer (SEE PAGE 14)

Pray the closing prayer now or after *lectio divina*.

Lectio Divina (SEE PAGE 7)

Relax your body and maintain a posture of prayer (back straight, eyes shut, feet flat on the floor). This exercise can take as long as you want, but in the context of this Bible study, 10 to 20 minutes should be sufficient.

The meditations that follow are provided only to help group participants use this prayer form, but note that *lectio* is intended to bring one to a place of prayerful contemplation where the Word of God speaks to the hearer from his or her heart. (See page 7 for further instruction.)

The transfiguration of Jesus (17:1–8)

The transfiguration of Jesus transfigures our view of the world. In many ways, we have all experienced a transfiguration of our view of the world in our prayer, especially in moments of reflection. In the midst of prayer, when we suddenly experience God's presence in a real and unique manner, we find ourselves on that mountain with Jesus. The presence of God overshadows us, and we suddenly become more aware of the magnificence of Jesus in our lives and in creation.

✠ *What can I learn from this passage?*

The coming of Elijah (17:9–13)

Just as the deep experience of God in prayer can end quickly when we confront the difficulties of life, so the disciples of Jesus come "down from the mountain" with Jesus. They are confronted immediately with Jesus' discussion about death and resurrection and about the suffering of John the Baptist and Jesus' own suffering. The confusing part of experiencing an intimate moment with Christ in prayer is that within a short period of time we can be confronted with the struggles and distractions of our daily life here on Earth.

✠ *What can I learn from this passage?*

Jesus heals a possessed boy (17:14–23)

The disciples of Jesus have been without his presence for a short period of time, but it was long enough to weaken their faith. They were attempting to perform this exorcism on their own power, forgetting that all they have comes from God. Living with faith is difficult. We often have difficulty recalling the presence of God when the demons of the world surround us.

✠ *What can I learn from this passage?*

Paying the temple tax (17:24–27)

In our own society, people must pay taxes, but they may feel that some of their taxes are used to support immoral decisions or wars they deem to be unjust. Despite this, most Church leaders in many nations urge their members to be faithful citizens by paying their taxes. Besides some taxes being used for immoral purposes, most of the money is used for the moral good of society. Most religious leaders today would view paying taxes as a sign of good citizenship.

✠ *What can I learn from this passage?*

The greatest in the reign of God (18:1–5)

A very successful but humble writer wrote that he followed a dictum of Saint Teresa of Avila, which said that humility is truth. If God has given us great gifts, we should not be ashamed to speak of them when necessary, but we can never use these gifts to look down on others. According to Jesus, we should be as humble and dependent as children and should be welcoming to everyone, whether society considers a person to be lowly or powerful.

✠ *What can I learn from this passage?*

Avoiding temptation (18:6–14)

Jesus, aware that conflicts will arise among his followers, warns them not to confuse or reject those who are new to accepting his message. We have similar confrontations in the Church today. When new converts come into the Church, they should be nourished in the faith and not brought into the conflicts encountered by those who are more seasoned in the faith. Jesus continues to put mercy and compassion before all else.

✠ *What can I learn from this passage?*

Norms for correcting another (18:15–20)

Jesus encourages private prayer and public prayer. Jesus himself prayed in private and in public. He went off to a lonely place to pray, and he prayed in the synagogues on the Sabbath. Our private prayers lead us to public prayer, whether that public prayer be in a prayer group or in the celebration of the Eucharist.

✠ *What can I learn from this passage?*

Forgiveness (18:21–35)

A man who was dying said on his deathbed that he could not forgive his former wife for getting drunk and dropping their daughter on her head when she was a child, causing their daughter to have emotional and physical problems for the rest of her life. He did say, however, that despite his feelings, he prayed each day for his former wife. This was the only forgiveness he had to offer. God has forgiven our huge debt, but many must still admit that forgiveness is a constant struggle.

✠ *What can I learn from this passage?*

PART 2: INDIVIDUAL STUDY (MATTHEW 19—20)

Jesus continues to teach his disciples as he leads them on the journey toward Jerusalem and the cross. In Jerusalem, Jesus asserts his authority through a series of confrontations with the religious leaders.

Day 1: Divorce (19:1–12)

Matthew begins this section with the usual transition that tells of Jesus ending his discourse and moving on to a new area. The area now becomes significant because Jesus moves from Galilee, where his message has been accepted, to Judea, where he meets opposition and rejection. Matthew continues to show a split between the crowds who follow Jesus and the religious leaders who oppose him.

The Pharisees draw Jesus into a debate concerning divorce. Moses allowed divorce and decreed that a written notice of dismissal be given to the wife at the time of the divorce. (See Deuteronomy 24:1.) The debate did not dispute the right of divorce but, rather, the reason for the divorce. One group believed a divorce could be given for any reason at all, while the other group believed it could only be given in the case of adultery.

Jesus recalls the law of God at the beginning of creation. God created human beings as male and female, and the two become one flesh according to God's plan of creation. He sides with no one in this debate as he flatly states that divorce is never permitted. Jesus claims a divorced man as well as a divorced woman commits adultery if either one remarries. This judgment astounds the crowd (including the disciples), who believed divorce was allowed. Jesus claims Moses gave the law because of the stubbornness of the people. Because the people would not change their practice of divorcing a wife, the law was given to protect the woman. Through a notice of divorce, others would know a woman was no longer married. The law of God concerning the two becoming one precedes the law of Moses and is the true law.

As he does in the Sermon on the Mount, Jesus makes an exception for unlawful marriage. Many commentators see this as a reference to the prohibition against marrying a close relative, as found in the Book of

Leviticus (18:6–18). When the disciples hear Jesus' words, they declare it is better not to marry than to shackle oneself with such a strict law. Jesus admits the difficulty involved in his teaching, and he lists three categories of those who refrain from sexual relations. Some refrain due to physical disability; others, made eunuchs at some time in their lives, are unable to have sexual relations; some have freely chosen to renounce sexual relations for the sake of the kingdom. Although this last practice was not common during the time of Jesus, records show that members of the Essene community near the Dead Sea had chosen to practice celibacy. At the time Matthew wrote his gospel, some in the early Church had chosen celibacy for the sake of the reign of God.

Lectio Divina

Spend 8 to 10 minutes in silent contemplation of the following passage:

> Jesus does not choose such an apparently inflexible position about divorce to condemn those who are divorced, but he wishes to protect God's plan for creation. Jesus notes that the two become one, meaning they are more closely united with each other than they are with their own parents and siblings. In the beginning, God made the two one and told them to "Be fertile and multiply" (Genesis 1:28.) Jesus' law is for the family as well as for the couple. Divorce is not only difficult for the man and woman, but it is difficult for the whole family.

✠ *What can I learn from this passage?*

Day 2: Jesus Blesses the Children (19:13–15)

During the time of Jesus, people would bring their children to a rabbi, seeking a blessing for their children. The people recognize Jesus as a great and holy teacher, and they bring their children to him for such a blessing. The irritation of the disciples becomes the occasion for a further lesson about the kingdom. The disciples should not hinder the children, because the kingdom of heaven is made up of people with a childlike spirit of dependence on God. Like the little children, the disciples have no rights of their own, but only those given to them by God.

Lectio Divina

Spend 8 to 10 minutes in silent contemplation of the following passage:

> A day-care center in a small town advertised for elderly volunteers to sit with the babies at the center and play with them as surrogate grandparents. Several men and women volunteered and were soon deeply involved in their ministry. One day the manager of the day-care center pointed to the elderly men and women smiling broadly and playing with the giggling babies and said to one of the other workers at the center, "When you see this, you have to wonder who the real children are." Caring for others with the simplicity of a child, like the surrogate grandparents did, illustrates the reality that all people have a childlike simplicity when they reach out to help others.

✠ *What can I learn from this passage?*

Day 3: The Rich Young Man (19:16–30)

Although Matthew makes use of Mark's Gospel in the story of the rich young man, he makes some significant changes. When the man addresses Jesus as "good" in the Gospel of Mark (10:17–18), Jesus objects that he should not be called "good," because only God should be addressed in this way. Matthew, in his great respect for Jesus, softens the message, avoiding any comparison between Jesus and the "One who is good." Jesus directs the young man to live the commandments, naming five of them, along with the command to love one's neighbor as oneself. When the young man admits to keeping these commandments, Jesus calls him to a more perfect offering of his life and tells him to give all he has to the poor. Matthew omits the passage from Mark that has Jesus look upon the man with love. The man, unable to part with his riches, sadly leaves Jesus.

When Jesus tells his disciples that it is difficult for a rich person to enter heaven, they are surprised. To the people of Jesus' day, the gift of wealth was seen as a sign of God's favor. When Jesus tells his disciples that it is easier for a camel to pass through the eye of a needle than for a rich person to enter heaven, he exaggerates greatly to show the difficulty the rich face in entering heaven. The gifts of God, however, abound and overcome all impossibility, thus making it possible for a rich person to enter the kingdom of God.

Peter again speaks on behalf of the disciples when he asks what awaits those who have given up everything to follow Jesus. Jesus speaks of the Final Judgment where he (the glorified Son of Man) and the Twelve will sit as judges for the new Israel. Those who have given up everything for Jesus will receive a greater reward and will share in the joy of eternal life. The last line of this passage causes some difficulty. It does not seem to fit the message. If we place it in the context of the previous narrative, it would mean that many who are first (the rich) will be last, and many who are last (the disciples who left all) will be first in the kingdom of God.

Lectio Divina

Spend 8 to 10 minutes in silent contemplation of the following passage:

> In the story of the rich man, we have an example of a good man being possessed by his wealth. Many of us, without realizing it, could have the same problem. We may protect our time, refuse to use our talents to the extent we should, or protect our wealth. Jesus is not saying it is bad to be rich; he is saying how difficult it is for people of wealth to make the reign of God on Earth the center of their lives. But Jesus offers words of encouragement, namely, that all things are possible with God. The generous poor and the generous rich live together in the reign of God, each with their own challenges.

✠ *What can I learn from this passage?*

Day 4: The Laborers in the Vineyard (20:1–16)

The story of the laborers in the vineyard appears only in the Gospel of Matthew. Jesus tells his listeners that the kingdom of heaven is like a vineyard owner who went out several times during the day to hire workers for his vineyard. He promises those he hires first that he will pay them the usual daily wage. He goes out at mid-morning, noon, and mid-afternoon, and sends other laborers into his vineyard with the promise that he will pay them whatever is fair. At the end of the day, the owner begins by paying the last ones hired and gives them the same daily wage as those hired earlier in the day. When those hired first come to receive their wage, they expect more, and they grumble when they receive only the daily wage. The owner, however, believes he is being fair to those who worked all day and generous to those who worked only a few hours. The message reminds us that the kingdom of heaven is a gift that we do not merit no matter how long we work for it. The gift of the kingdom comes from the generosity of God.

The addition of the statement that the first shall be last and the last shall be first adds a new dimension to the story. Matthew could be addressing the people of his own day who were trying to understand how the Gentiles received so many of the gifts of Christianity while the Jews missed the coming of the Messiah. The fact that the Jewish nation had all those centuries of preparation did not guarantee they would automatically recognize the Messiah when he came. Even though the Gentiles come to understand the message of the kingdom late in creation, they still gain the fullness of the gift of the kingdom of heaven.

Lectio Divina

Spend 8 to 10 minutes in silent contemplation of the following passage:

> In God's generosity, the good thief who repented at the last hour of his life could have as high a place in God's eternal glory as Saint Peter. What seems unfair to us is fair to God, and we should rejoice that all our brothers and sisters in our human family have an opportunity to share in God's glory, even if they worked at it for a shorter time than we did.

✠ *What can I learn from this passage?*

Day 5: Third Prediction of the Passion and Resurrection (20:17–19)

The third prediction of the passion becomes even more dramatic and detailed than the two before it. As Jesus begins his journey toward Jerusalem, he takes the Twelve aside to tell them that he (the Son of Man) will be handed over to the chief priests and scribes who will condemn him and to the Gentiles (the Romans) who will ridicule, flog, and crucify him. Whenever Jesus speaks of his passion and death, he always adds the fact of his resurrection. He tells his disciples that he will be raised up on the third day.

Lectio Divina

Spend 8 to 10 minutes in silent contemplation of the following passage:

> This third prediction of Jesus' passion, death, and resurrection reminds us that the destiny of Jesus must have been on his mind always. If we knew we were going to endure a horrible death, how would we feel during life? Jesus' passion and death were not only dreaded when Jesus was praying through his agony in the garden, but he had to live with the thought throughout his ministry. This must have been a great agony of anticipation for him, yet he endured it for love of us.

✠ *What can I learn from this passage?*

Day 6: Discipleship and Healings (20:20–34)

In the Gospel of Mark (10:35–37), James and John approach Jesus, requesting places of honor in the kingdom. Matthew has the mother of James and John make the request. Jesus tells her she does not understand what she is asking, and he asks if they can drink of the cup he is to drink from. The idea of the cup of suffering is used often in the Scriptures. When they agree they can drink of the cup, Jesus tells them they will do so, but that the right to determine who sits in a place of honor in the kingdom belongs to his Father alone.

The other disciples, not understanding the kingdom, grow jealous of James and John, and Jesus must teach them a lesson concerning the kingdom. The pagan Gentiles look for worldly domination over others, but those who rule in the kingdom of God must choose the path of the servant spoken of in the prophecy of Isaiah (53:11). The true ruler in the kingdom must serve others. The Son of Man (Jesus as the Messiah) comes to serve and to give his life as a "ransom" for many. The true ruler in the kingdom of God must follow the example of Jesus.

Matthew follows the story of ambition with the story of two blind men who call after Jesus. In calling his disciples to a life of service, Jesus opens their eyes to what it means to be a disciple. The story follows a similar one in the Gospel of Mark (10:46–52). Matthew tells of two blind men, whereas Mark names only one, a man named Bartimaeus. The two men call Jesus as though they are praying, using the messianic title of "Son of David" and the faith title of "Lord." The early Church community used this expression to identify the risen Christ, the Son of God. Although they are physically blind, the two men have the sight of faith. Jesus forces them to state their request, although it would have seemed obvious to anyone in the crowd. Jesus, filled with compassion, gives them their sight, and they become his followers. The simple statement that these men became followers of Jesus could illustrate that the crowd is beginning to grow as Jesus nears the moment of his triumphal entry into Jerusalem.

Lectio Divina

Spend 8 to 10 minutes in silent contemplation of the following passage:

Blessed Teresa of Calcutta encouraged her sisters to work as though they were caring for Christ. One new arrival worked for three hours washing a man who had fallen into a drain some time before and who was covered with wounds, dirt, and maggots. She came back with a brilliant smile on her face and said to Mother Teresa that she had been touching the body of Christ for three hours. She was not blind to the presence of Christ in this person.

✠ *What can I learn from this passage?*

Review Questions

1. Why was Jesus so concerned about marriage and divorce?
2. Why did Jesus say it is hard for a rich person to enter the kingdom of heaven?
3. What is the message of the parable of the workers in the vineyard?
4. What is the message of the healing of the two blind men?

LESSON 8

Ministry in Jerusalem

MATTHEW 21—23

You shall love the Lord your God with all your heart, with all your soul, and with all your mind. This is the greatest and the first commandment. The second is like it: You shall love your neighbor as yourself (22:37–39).

Opening Prayer (SEE PAGE 14)

Context

Part 1: Matthew 21—22:14 Jesus enters Jerusalem, and his presence becomes visible as he enters riding on a donkey and accepting the homage of the people. He recognizes his dignity and authority as the Son of God and dares to challenge the cheating merchants in the Temple. Because he acts with such authority, the religious leaders will seek to kill him. Jesus infuriates the religious leaders as he compares them to those who say they will obey but who do not. Through parables, he compares them to unjust tenants and to those who were rejected because they refused to come to the banquet of the son.

Part 2: Matthew 22:15—23:39 Jesus again confronts the religious leaders. They attempt to trap Jesus in his speech with questions about the payment of taxes to Caesar and the resurrection of the dead, but he outwits them. He teaches the greatest commandment is love, but he must denounce the scribes and the Pharisees for their hypocritical actions. Jesus sadly laments over his beloved Jerusalem.

PART 1: GROUP STUDY (MATTHEW 21—22:14)

Read aloud Matthew 21—22:14

21:1–11 Triumphal entry into Jerusalem

Matthew presents a more triumphant entry into Jerusalem than does Mark. He gives directions to his disciples at Bethphage, which is on the slope of the Mount of Olives. The prophet Zechariah saw the Lord as coming from the east (14:4), which is the direction from which Jesus would approach Jerusalem. The importance of the moment is heightened by the manner in which Jesus tells his disciples to prepare for his entrance. Because it is the time ordained by God, no one will stop them. Matthew sees the entry into Jerusalem as foretold by two Old Testament prophecies. In Isaiah 62:11, word is sent to "daughter Zion," and in Zechariah 9:9, the Lord will come "on a donkey, on a colt," which are humble beasts of burden. The reference to these animals was actually meant to be a reference to only one animal, spoken of in two different ways. Matthew misunderstood the prophecy to mean two animals. The disciples did as Jesus told them and placed their cloaks on the animals as a sign of homage to Jesus.

The feast being celebrated at the time was most likely the feast of Tabernacles, which included the carrying of palm branches. During the feast, Psalm 118 is recited. This psalm becomes the cry of the people as Jesus enters Jerusalem. They praise Jesus as the Son of David, "who comes in the name of the LORD" (118:26). A large crowd, laying their cloaks and palm branches on the ground, greets Jesus as he enters Jerusalem. Just as the whole city of Jerusalem was stirred up at the news of the birth of Jesus, so now the whole city is stirred up as his ministry draws to a close.

21:12–17 Jesus cleanses the Temple

Because Jesus is truly the Messiah, his first point of business in Jerusalem is going to the Temple, the sacred center of Judaism and Jerusalem. Because the Greek and Roman coin was used in the daily trade of the people, they carried this coin with them. The coin that belonged to a foreign ruler and the secular world had no place in the Temple, so the people had to exchange this coin for the Temple coin. Merchants just inside the

Temple precincts exchanged this coin for the people, and they also sold the necessary animals for sacrifice. Some of them apparently cheated the people in this exchange. Jesus, as the messianic guardian of the house of God, overturns the tables of the merchants, proclaiming in the words of Isaiah (56:7) that the house of God is called a "house of prayer"; he follows with words from Jeremiah (7:11), which proclaim that the people have made God's house a "den of thieves."

Jesus cures the outcasts and those who are blind and lame in the Temple area. The chief priest and scribes become enraged that Jesus should perform such healings within the Temple and that the people should hail him as the "Son of David." The learned leaders view the people as not being well educated and therefore gullible to Jesus' message and mission. Jesus responds to the concern of the leaders by quoting from an Old Testament psalm (8:2–3) that describes a hymn of praise coming from infants and children. Jesus quietly withdraws to the nearby village of Bethany, east of Jerusalem, and spends the night there.

21:18–22 Cursing of the fig tree

The story of Jesus cursing the fig tree is a parable in action. The fig tree represents Judaism. The fig tree has nothing on it except leaves. Since it does not bear proper fruit, Jesus curses it, and it withers and dies. In the Gospel of Mark (11:12–14), the fig tree represents Israel. Matthew changes the point of the story to show the power of prayer and faith. Jesus' disciples are stunned when they see the immediate shriveling of the tree. Jesus tells them that the person who has faith in prayer can perform actions similar to throwing a mountain into the sea. In prayer, the person of faith will receive whatever he or she seeks.

21:23–27 By what authority?

The role of the chief priests and the elders become more prominent in the Gospel of Matthew as Jesus nears his passion and death. They question Jesus concerning the authority for his activities in the Temple. Jesus faces this first of several confrontations in the debate format used by the rabbis of his day. He answers the questions of the chief priests and elders with a question of his own, a technique used by the rabbis of Jesus' day.

To understand the source of Jesus' authority, they would have to understand the source of the authority of John the Baptist, so Jesus asks them the source of John's call to baptize. The leaders know they will condemn themselves despite the answer they must give. To say that John's baptism comes from God would lead the people to ask why they rejected John in the past, and to deny that John's baptism comes from God would place them in opposition to the people who believe John was sent by God. Rather than answer Jesus' question, they plead ignorance. Jesus, recognizing their evasion as a refusal to answer, refuses to answer their questions.

21:28–32 Parable of the two sons

In the first of three parables, Jesus tells the story of two sons whose father sends them to work in the vineyard. This parable is found only in the Gospel of Matthew. The first son refuses to go but changes his mind, while the second son agrees to go into the vineyard but does not go. The parable ends with Jesus asking the religious leaders to decide which of the two sons was true to the father. A common way of ending a parable was with a question that had an obvious answer. In this way, the parable had the double effect of teaching a lesson and having those toward whom the parable was directed clearly apply the parable to themselves. The chief priests and elders must answer that the son who actually went into the vineyard was the one who did the father's will.

The religious leaders recognized that the second son who said he would do what the father wanted represents them and their promise to do what God asked of them without ever doing it. The first son represents the tax collectors and prostitutes who rejected God at first but then reformed their lives at the preaching of John. Even when the leaders of the people saw the great effects of John's preaching, they still refused to repent and believe in him.

21:33–46 Parable of the wicked tenants

The story of the vineyard recalls many of the images used by Isaiah. (See 5:1–7.) In the story, the owner of the vineyard is God. The tenants of the vineyard represent Israel, while the slaves who come to collect the earnings for the owner are the prophets. The tenants (Israel) punish and even kill the slaves (the prophets). The owner decides to send his son (Jesus).

In the Gospel of Mark (12:1–12), the son is killed inside the vineyard, and his body is thrown out of the vineyard. Matthew corrects Mark and has the son dragged out of the vineyard (Jerusalem) before he is killed. Jesus, like the son in the parable, is dragged outside Jerusalem before he is crucified. Jesus again has his listeners pass judgment on the case when he asks them what the owner will do to the tenants. When the leaders of the people answer that the owner will destroy the tenants and lease the vineyard to others (Gentiles), Jesus quotes from the Old Testament psalm (118:22) that speaks of the rejected stone as the cornerstone of the structure. Jesus is the cornerstone that, when rejected by Israel, leaves Israel to its own destruction. Jesus will become the cornerstone of the new structure of the Church. The leaders again recognize that this parable is directed at them. If they had not feared the crowds who considered Jesus a prophet, they would have arrested him.

22:1–14 The wedding banquet

A favorite image of the messianic age used in the Old Testament was that of a wedding banquet. Jesus uses this image in his parable about the banquet that is ready for the guests. The messianic age has arrived, and the king (God) is giving a wedding banquet for his son (Jesus). He sends out his servants (the prophets) to tell the invited guests (the Israelites) that the banquet is ready (the messianic age has arrived). When the invited guests reject the invitation, and even kill some of the servants, the king sends out his army to destroy these people. This recalls the destruction of Jerusalem that occurred in the year 70, and so is still fresh in the minds of Matthew's audience. The king again sends out his servants, who now invite everyone they meet—sinners and outcasts as well as good people. These people are the new Israel, and they fill the banquet hall.

Matthew adds another parable to the story of the banquet and makes one parable out of two. When the king comes into the banquet, he finds a man not properly dressed for the celebration, and he has him bound and thrown out. The members of the early Church realize that some who belong to their number are not living as true disciples of Jesus. They have not acted properly for the privilege of sharing in the banquet of the kingdom. Just because they have accepted the invitation to the banquet does not automatically give them a right to ignore the commands of Jesus concerning those who live in the kingdom. The passage ends with a statement that implies many are invited to share in the kingdom, but those who accept are few.

Review Questions

1. What message do we learn from Jesus' triumphal entry into Jerusalem?
2. What is significant about Jesus' act of cleansing the Temple?
3. What was the aim of Jesus' parable about the two sons going into the vineyard?
4. What is the message found in the story of the unjust tenants in the vineyard?
5. What message does Jesus wish to teach in his story of the king who hosts a wedding banquet for his son?

Closing Prayer (SEE PAGE 14)

Pray the closing prayer now or after *lectio divina*.

Lectio Divina (SEE PAGE 7)

Relax your body and maintain a posture of prayer (back straight, eyes shut, feet flat on the floor). This exercise can take as long as you want, but in the context of this Bible study, 10 to 20 minutes should be sufficient.

The meditations that follow are provided only to help group participants use this prayer form, but note that *lectio* is intended to bring one to a place of prayerful contemplation where the Word of God speaks to the hearer from his or her heart. (See page 7 for further instruction.)

Triumphal entry into Jerusalem (21:1–11)

Jesus knows that the same people who praise him at this time may call for his crucifixion later. Stories abound about people who were once pious followers of Jesus but who later abandoned him, choosing to ignore or deny his existence as the Son of God. We have received the gift of faith, but we must keep in contact with Christ through prayer and good deeds. Faith, like love, does not stand still. It either grows or diminishes.

✠ *What can I learn from this passage?*

Jesus cleanses the Temple (21:12–17)

When Jesus chases out the money exchangers and merchants, he is not saying religious articles or other items pertaining to the worshiping community cannot be sold in its gathering area. His anger is over the sinful cheating taking place. The Temple is where God visits with God's assembled people. Jesus reminds us that we should treat our sacred space with reverence.

✠ *What can I learn from this passage?*

Cursing of the fig tree (21:18–22)

Many people view prayer as a type of one-sided contract between them and God. "God, I prayed, now you have to answer me." After all, Jesus promised to answer our prayers. We know, however, that faith in prayer means faith in God. God will keep God's side of the bargain, but God will also determine what that is. We pray, and our faith tells us to trust that God is answering our prayer in some manner, even if we do not see the answer.

✠ *What can I learn from this passage?*

By what authority? (21:23–27)

Our mind must always be open to the authority of Jesus as found in the Scriptures. The gospels are a different type of story for those with faith than it is for those without faith. Those without faith may consider Jesus to be a courageous person who preaches about love, but they reject stories of his miracles as fiction. For them, Jesus does not have divine authority. For us, Jesus is God become human, and Jesus speaks with the authority of God.

✠ *What can I learn from this passage?*

Parable of the two sons (21:28–32)

Saint Thomas Becket is a good example of a "no" becoming a "yes." He was a friend of the king who made him a powerful archbishop of Canterbury, believing that Becket would be a staunch ally against the pope and the Church in England. Thomas, however, changed and became a champion of the Church, despite the knowledge that he would most likely be assassinated. Thomas was eventually murdered by three men who considered themselves loyal to the king. When he was dying, it is reported that he said, "I wish I had served my God as well as I served my king." His "no" to the vineyard of the Church in his earlier life became a "yes" in his later years. It is never too late to change a "no" to a "yes."

✠ *What can I learn from this passage?*

Parable of the wicked tenants (21:33–46)

As Christians, we are the new tenants in God's vineyard. Unlike the tenants in the story, we must produce good fruit and return it to the Lord. While working in the Lord's vineyard, we can expect to encounter weeds that demand our hard work in uprooting them. God gave us a garden, but God did not promise us a rose garden. The gift is that we are placed in the vineyard of the Lord here on Earth. The difficulty is that we must work hard to produce fruit. The joy is that we work and produce fruit for a loving God.

✠ *What can I learn from this passage?*

The wedding banquet (22:1–14)

The story tells us that the king invites the good as well as the bad. This means that in the reign of God, we will find those who are good and those who are bad. The one who does not wear a wedding garment is the one who comes to the banquet with no intention of changing his or her life. The "party pooper" is thrown out. Enjoying the banquet means we add something to the party. We pray together, believe together, and strive to live as good a life as possible, not for ourselves alone, but for the king and all the other people sharing in the banquet.

✠ *What can I learn from this passage?*

Part 2: Individual Study (Matthew 22:15—23:39)

Human beings are made in the image and likeness of God. Just as a coin of the empire in Jesus' day bore the image of Caesar and belonged to him, so we belong to God. Jesus continually warns his listeners not to follow the example of the scribes and Pharisees, whom Jesus describes as hypocrites because their internal attitudes do not match their external appearance as pious leaders.

Day 1: Paying Taxes to Caesar (22:15–22)

The Pharisees and the Herodians could hardly be called allies during the time of Jesus. The Pharisees resisted foreign domination, and the Herodians supported it. Both joined forces, however, to question Jesus concerning the paying of taxes to the emperor. Matthew portrays these groups as flattering Jesus with insincere words of praise. They are actually trying to trap him. If Jesus agrees to pay the tax, he will appear to support a foreign ruler. If Jesus refuses to pay the tax, the Herodians can accuse him of undermining the rule of Rome. Jesus recognizes their hypocrisy and asks them for a coin used to pay the taxes. In a subtle manner, Matthew has the religious leaders and the Herodians produce the coin instead of Jesus. Jesus, following the belief of his day that any material goods belonged to the one whose image was somehow embedded in that material, applies this way of thinking to the Roman coin. As long as Caesar's image is there, it belongs to Caesar.

Jesus actually speaks of repayment, as though the coin is something borrowed or taken from Caesar that should eventually be returned to him. The same is true of God. God has blessed creation with the imprint of God. Creation is made in the image and likeness of God. Repayment to God means recognizing God's dominion over all and repaying by remaining faithful to God. Jesus again outwits his enemies, who then leave him.

Lectio Divina

Spend 8 to 10 minutes in silent contemplation of the following passage:

The first chapters of the Bible tell us that we are made in the image and likeness of God. When Jesus states that the coin, because it has the image of Caesar, belongs to Caesar, he is saying we must live in a world full of images foreign to the image of God. We enjoy some of the gifts of creation and use them as God wishes, but we also have other aspects of creation that attempt to lure us away from God. When we encounter these temptations, we can remember that we bear the image and likeness of God and therefore must act as a true likeness of God's love.

✠ *What can I learn from this passage?*

Day 2: The Sadducees and Resurrection (22:23–33)

The Sadducees accepted only the first five books of the Scriptures as authentic. Because these books made no reference to the resurrection from the dead, the Sadducees refused to believe in resurrection. As proof of the absurdity of belief in resurrection, the Sadducees quote from the Book of Deuteronomy (25:5–10), one of the first five books. The Sadducees believed Moses gave the Levirate law, which states that a man must marry his deceased brother's widow. They pose a problem about seven brothers, each of whom marries the same woman before he dies. They ask which of the seven brothers will be considered her husband after the resurrection.

Jesus faults the Pharisees' question on two counts. They misunderstand the meaning of resurrection, which involves a different type of existence in which marriage does not exist and in which people live as angels in heaven. Jesus then quotes from the Book of Exodus, again one of the first five books of the Old Testament, in which God proclaims, "I am...the God of Abraham, the God of Isaac, and the God of Jacob" (3:6). Because God is the God of the living and not the dead, these patriarchs must have been living at the time God addressed Moses. In this way, Jesus tells the Sadducees that the resurrection is indeed implied in one of the first five books of the Scriptures. Jesus' answer astounds the crowd.

Lectio Divina

Spend 8 to 10 minutes in silent contemplation of the following passage:

Resurrection from the dead is a central point of Christian belief. We believe Jesus was raised from the dead, and we believe we will also be raised from the dead because Jesus said we would. We do expect that resurrection from the dead will take place for each one of us and that we will exist forever. What form that will take is a mystery. We also expect that resurrection will be a state of eternal joy and love in union with God for those who have remained faithful to God to death. The thought of resurrection gives us hope in life and hope in dying. Resurrection is a promise and a gift that comes to us through the words of Jesus.

✠ *What can I learn from this passage?*

Day 3: The Greatest Commandment (22:34–40)

The Pharisees now come forward to engage Jesus in a controversy concerning the greatest commandment. The rabbis of the day often tried to summarize the more than six hundred laws of Judaism into one single commandment. A lawyer from among the Pharisees speaks on their behalf and asks Jesus to state which law is the greatest. Jesus quotes from two Old Testament books for his answer. He tells them they must love the Lord their God with all their heart, soul, and mind (Deuteronomy 6:5), and they must love their neighbor as themselves (Leviticus 19:18). The answer given by Jesus is not new, but it is the first time someone has linked the two laws of love together. Love of neighbor is now seen in a different light as it is joined with the command concerning love of God.

Lectio Divina

Spend 8 to 10 minutes in silent contemplation of the following passage:

Jesus tells us to love God with all our heart, soul, and mind, and he adds that we should love our neighbor as ourselves. In resurrection, we move into a culture where love of God, neighbor, and self are dominant. We are meant to spend our lives on Earth attempting to reach that kind of love, and somewhere between death and resurrection, we meet the searing look of Christ and suddenly understand what real love means. At that moment, we are prepared to live an eternity of love with God, neighbor, and self.

✠ *What can I learn from this passage?*

Day 4: The Questions About David's Son (22:41–46)

The leaders of the people no longer challenge Jesus, so Jesus now challenges them. Jesus asks them to tell him about the Messiah when he asks, "Whose son is he?" When they answer that the Messiah is to come as a Son of David, Jesus poses a problem for them. The people of Jesus' day believed a father was greater than his son and that an ancestor was greater than any of his descendants. They also believed David was the author of all the psalms. Jesus asks how David, who wrote the psalms under the influence of the Holy Spirit, could call the Messiah one of his offspring, by the title *Lord,* as he does in Psalm 110. The Pharisees are not able to answer this question and, in silent humiliation, ask Jesus no further questions.

The message Matthew puts on the lips of Jesus in this section may have originated in the early Church rather than during the time of Jesus. The members of the early Church had a much clearer idea of Jesus as Lord than did the people who lived during the time of Jesus. For the reader of the Gospel of Matthew, the answer to the question was known. Jesus was the Lord, the Son of God.

Lectio Divina

Spend 8 to 10 minutes in silent contemplation of the following passage:

As great as David was, he was still created by God. Jesus, as the Son of God, was the Lord of David. For those of us today who believe Jesus is God, this is no mystery. Jesus, the Lord of all creation, became human and dwelt among us.

✠ *What can I learn from this passage?*

Day 5: Jesus Confronts the Scribes and Pharisees (23:1–12)

The major part of this passage comes from the M tradition, which Matthew alone uses as a source. The scribes and Pharisees follow in the tradition of Moses; they have the duty of interpreting and teaching the Law and the prophets. Jesus does not reject or challenge this right, but he does warn the people against following the example of these leaders. Although Jesus urges the people to follow what the Pharisees teach, he accuses the leaders of speaking boldly and of placing burdens on others that they themselves refuse to bear. As hypocrites, they perform their actions with an external flourish meant to gain admiration. In Jesus' day, the Pharisees wore tiny boxes on their foreheads and wrists that held scrolls of the Scriptures. These ornaments were called *phylacteries,* and the scribes and Pharisees would make them large as a sign of their great love for the Scriptures. The tassel of their cloaks signified their dedication to holiness—the longer the tassel, the greater the sign of devotion. Jesus condemns the scribes and Pharisees for these external signs of holiness.

When they went to banquets or took their places in the synagogues, these leaders sought the places of honor. They even gloried in titles of honor, such as rabbi, father, or teacher. Jesus warns against the use of these titles, not because they are wrong in themselves, but because of the meaning attributed to some of them. One teaches, others learn—but God alone is the true Father, and Jesus, as the Messiah, is the true teacher. The real place of honor belongs to the person who humbly serves others. Besides having a value for the crowds who must deal with the scribes and Pharisees, the message also has value for the community for which Matthew is writing. A Church structure is developing, and this message serves as a reminder that the true leader of the community is the one who serves.

Lectio Divina

Spend 8 to 10 minutes in silent contemplation of the following passage:

Jesus has an eternal view of life. From this viewpoint, it is ridiculous to seek recognition from people here on Earth for our deeds. Two hundred years from now, people may not know who we were or what we did, but that does not matter. What matters is that we used God's gifts in a way that may still be having a good influence on the lives of many in the future.

✠ *What can I learn from this passage?*

Day 6: Jesus' Woes and Laments (23:13–39)

A *woe* was originally a lamentation over the dead, and Jesus uses *woe* here to express the fact that the scribes and Pharisees are spiritually dead. The woes express grief over some condition that exists and the outcome that will follow.

The first woe bemoans the fact that the scribes and Pharisees have rejected the kingdom of heaven in rejecting the message of Jesus, and that they use their energies to keep others from entering the kingdom because of this rejection.

The second woe laments the great energy the Jewish leaders expend on their missionary activities while they convert and lead others to a greater evil. Matthew realizes this message applies to the members of the early Church who are converts from Judaism. The early Jewish Christians seek converts to Christianity, but they impose the heavy burdens of Jewish customs on these new converts and make their condition worse than before their conversion.

The third woe laments that the religious leaders reject oaths made on that which is most sacred, such as the Temple, the altar, and God, and place the strength of an oath on the gold in the Temple, on the gift on the altar, or on heaven itself. They are blind guides because they place the strength of an oath over the lesser good. Although Jesus, in an earlier section of the gospel, spoke against taking oaths of any kind, he has a different intention here. He is stating that those who do take oaths should realize that all oaths are sacred.

In the fourth woe, Jesus condemns the scribes and Pharisees for the time spent on calculating the religious taxes on goods from their fields while neglecting the more important matters such as justice, mercy, and faith. They spend their time on the smaller things (straining out the gnat) while neglecting the more important (swallowing the camel). In doing this they show that they are blind guides who do not truly understand the Law.

The fifth woe likens the Pharisees to a cup that is clean on the outside and filthy on the inside. They are more concerned about their external appearance than about living the Law within themselves.

The sixth woe speaks a little more forcefully about the same hypocrisy. The tombs of the dead were whitewashed on the outside to give them the appearance of cleanliness, while within the tombs lay the decaying bodies of the dead. The religious leaders look virtuous on the outside, while they are filled with decay and evil on the inside.

The seventh and last woe rebukes the scribes and Pharisees who honor the prophets and saints of the past by decorating their tombs and proclaiming they would have treated these holy people differently had the scribes and Pharisees lived in the past. Jesus says they are actually no better than their ancestors, because they treat Jesus and his followers in the same manner. Jesus addresses them with the derogatory terms of *vipers* and *snakes,* names ordinarily reserved for pagans. In their treatment of Jesus and his followers, they are no better than pagans. Matthew is aware of the treatment received by the members of the early Church after the destruction of Jerusalem. He knows the Pharisees rejected Christ and persecuted his followers. Because they have done this, they will be responsible for all the blood shed throughout the total period of the Scriptures, beginning with the first shedding of blood (Abel in Genesis 4:1–16) to the death of the last prophet recorded in the Old Testament (Zechariah in 2 Chronicles 24:20–22).

Jesus laments over the city of Jerusalem, calling it the city that has killed the prophets. He also speaks of those who reject the ones who are sent, a reference to the disciples who are sent out by Jesus to preach. Matthew writes the gospel after the destruction of Jerusalem, and he has the advantage of looking back over the final fate of that city and the form of religious leadership following the destruction. While attempting to rebuild after the destruction, the Pharisees became powerful and persecuted the followers of Jesus, believing Jerusalem's destruction was the result of the contamination of Judaism by Christians.

In expressing his love for the people of Jerusalem, Jesus demonstrates his compassion by using the female image of a mother hen gathering her young under her wings. When he says they will not see him again until they proclaim, "Blessed is he who comes in the name of the Lord," he is apparently referring to his coming in glory.

Lectio Divina

Spend 8 to 10 minutes in silent contemplation of the following passage:

Jesus condemned sin in the gospels, but the sin he abhors most is the sin of hypocrisy. When people look perfect on the outside but are full of evil on the inside, they appear to be close to God, but they are actually far from God. Jesus did not come to condemn but to bring life. His lament over Jerusalem shows the great love God has for all people. We can ask ourselves if there is anything in our lives that would make Jesus lament over us. If so, we can always turn Jesus' lament into joy by living close to God.

✠ *What can I learn from this passage?*

Review Questions

1. What did Jesus mean when he said, "Then repay to Caesar what belongs to Caesar, and to God what belongs to God"?
2. What is the meaning of Jesus' answer to the question of resurrection from the dead for the Sadducees?
3. What did Jesus identify as the greatest commandment?
4. How could an offspring of David be greater than David?

LESSON 9

Tribulation and Judgment

MATTHEW 24–25

Therefore, stay awake! For you do not know on which day your Lord will come (24:42).

Opening Prayer (SEE PAGE 14)

Context

Part 1: Matthew 24:1–44 Jesus speaks of the destruction of the Temple and the coming of the last days. His message is known as the "eschatological discourse." The word *eschatological* comes from a Greek word, *eschaton,* which means "the end." The discourse may be divided into two parts, with the first part (Matthew 24:1–44) following Mark closely (Mark 13:1–37).

Part 2: Matthew 24:45—25 The author presents the second part of the eschatological discourse, which consists of a mixture of the Q source and the evangelist's own tradition (M). He presents two parables from Jesus, one that calls for those in the kingdom of heaven to be prepared for the coming of Jesus, and the second that challenges his listeners to use their talents as God wills. The discourse ends with a parable about judgment, in which those who serve Christ well will be rewarded (the sheep), and those who do not serve Christ well will be condemned (the goats).

PART 1: GROUP STUDY (MATTHEW 24:1–44)

Read aloud Matthew 24:1–44

24:1–14 *The beginning of the catastrophes*

The disciples of Jesus stand in awe before the magnificent Temple, and Jesus tells them that all this will be torn down and not one stone will stand upon another. The early community knew of the destruction of Jerusalem and the Temple, since it had already taken place at the time of the writing of the gospel. It also seems likely that Jesus foresaw some destruction of the Temple, because it was a major accusation brought against Jesus at his trial before the Sanhedrin. Jesus makes his statement definitive by saying, "Amen, I say to you...."

Jesus takes the position of authority as he again sits to teach his message. His presence at the foot of the Mount of Olives indicates again that he is the Messiah, because the prophet foretold that the Messiah would come from the Mount of Olives. (See Zechariah 14:4.) Matthew portrays the disciples as understanding the message of Jesus when they ask him privately when the destruction of the Temple will take place and what will signal the Second Coming and the end of the world. The disciples could hardly have understood this message about Jesus before his resurrection, since the reaction of the disciples during Jesus' passion would have seemed unlikely in the face of the disciples' knowledge of Jesus' Second Coming. Matthew is directing his message toward those reading his gospel in the year 85 and beyond.

Jesus tells his listeners to be on guard because of the temptation and turmoil that are to come. He warns about false prophets who will arise (and did arise right before the destruction of Jerusalem). Some will even claim to be the Messiah. The disciples of Jesus should not panic when they hear of wars and rumors of wars, because these things must happen before the end. The whole Earth will be shaken as nations war with one another, widespread famine and disease will prevail, and natural disasters will occur on the Earth. The disciples will undergo suffering and even death at the hands of the nations, and even the disciples will betray one another in this moment of trial. False prophets will rise up and lead many astray.

Some members of the early Church will lose their enthusiasm for the faith, and they will live a faith that is empty and cold. Throughout all of these difficulties faced by the early Church (the "birth pangs"), some individuals will hold firm and come to eternal life. Only after the Good News is preached to all nations will the end finally come.

24:15–28 Tribulation and confusion

The features of the destruction of Jerusalem and the end of the world are so closely linked that it is sometimes difficult to determine which event Jesus describes. In this passage, Jesus alludes to the destruction of Jerusalem. Jesus refers to Daniel (9:27, 11:31, 12:11), who foretold an abomination that deeply affected the lives of the Israelite people. This recalls an occasion around 168 BC when Antiochus IV, a foreign ruler who controlled Judea, placed an image of a pagan god within the Jewish Temple. This incident eventually triggered the revolt of the Maccabees, whose courage stirred the minds of the Jewish nation to fight for freedom for generations to come. Matthew has Jesus use this same image of abomination when he alludes to the invasion of the Romans, who destroy Jerusalem and the Temple. Before the invasion, Christians apparently received some warning to flee the Holy City.

The destruction of the city will be so severe that no one will have a chance to turn back even for a moment. The person on the rooftop and in the field should flee, not even taking time to venture back into their homes for some belongings or a cloak. The dangers to those nursing or pregnant, as well as the hardships that would come with winter weather, are obvious. Jesus urges the people to pray that these events will not take place when a person is experiencing difficulty. If the invasion takes place on the Sabbath, it will cause confusion for those who obediently limit their movement and work on that day of rest. For the sake of the chosen (the Christians), God will shorten the number of days until this takes place.

Jesus speaks about the era when messiahs and false prophets, because of their apparently miraculous powers, will lead even the chosen astray. Jesus believes his warning should remind them that this is meant to happen. Forewarned is forearmed. When the end finally comes, it will be so swift that no one will be able to foretell its immediate occurrence. The coming of the Son of Man (Christ in his glory) will be as swift as lightning. As sure as vultures gather around a dead body, so sure is the Second Coming of Christ, the Son of Man in his glory.

24:29–31 The coming of the Son of Man

Around the time of Jesus, a type of writing called apocalyptic literature was popular, and evangelists make use of this form of literature when speaking of the end of the world. Apocalyptic literature uses symbols and visions that describe in poetic and symbolic language revelations given by God. These visions usually speak of wars, great changes in the skies, angelic messengers, and judgment as Jesus does in this passage. A common mistake of many people, especially certain television evangelists, is to interpret the apocalyptic language in a literal way, as though it exactly describes the events we should expect at the end of the world.

The use of apocalyptic language becomes more intense as Jesus speaks of the Second Coming. Heavenly bodies (sun, moon, stars) will be shaken, and the Son of Man will come upon the clouds in his full glory. The angels will go forth with the usual apocalyptic trumpet blast that signifies a heavenly visitation, and they will gather the chosen from the four winds (the four ends of the Earth).

24:32–35 The lesson of the fig tree

As Jesus often does, he takes an image common to his audience and builds his message around it. Here he tells his listeners to learn a lesson from the fig tree. Using the image of the fig tree, Jesus reminds his listeners that they can predict summer by the emergence of new sprouts of vegetation on the tree. In the same way, they should realize the end is near when all those things he foretold take place. The members of the early Church expected the Second Coming to take place soon. This could account for the announcement that the present generation would not pass away until all these things take place. These words rose from the early preaching of the Church rather than from Jesus. Even after all is finished, the Word of God, which is eternal, will never end.

24:36–44 Be prepared

Not even the Son knows when Judgment Day will come; only the Father knows. Jesus tells his audience that Judgment Day, which consists of the coming of the Son of Man (Jesus in his glory), will be a surprise. When Jesus tells them it will be no different than it was in the days of Noah, he is not saying they will be sinning as the people were doing in the time of Noah, but that they will be going through the normal routines of daily life with no concern for the end. The end will come on an ordinary day in the lives of most people. Two men will be in the field and two women will be grinding. The idea of separating one from the other is a typical image used in the Gospel of Matthew to show that one would be chosen on Judgment Day and the other rejected. Because they cannot know the exact time of the Second Coming, people should be ready at all times.

Review Questions

1. What did Jesus say about the destruction of the Temple?
2. What should people do when the destruction of Jerusalem begins?
3. Why does Jesus use a fig tree to teach his lesson?
4. When will the day and the hour of destruction happen?

Closing Prayer (SEE PAGE 14)

Pray the closing prayer now or after *lectio divina.*

Lectio Divina (SEE PAGE 7)

Relax your body and maintain a posture of prayer (back straight, eyes shut, feet flat on the floor). This exercise can take as long as you want, but in the context of this Bible study, 10 to 20 minutes should be sufficient.

The meditations that follow are provided only to help group participants use this prayer form, but note that *lectio* is intended to bring one to a place of prayerful contemplation where the Word of God speaks to the hearer from his or her heart. (See page 7 for further instruction.)

The beginning of the catastrophes (24:1–14)

Although some people still have not heard about Jesus, his message has spread throughout most of the world, even to areas where atheistic governments attempt to squelch the message by killing those who practice or preach Christianity. God sent courageous missionaries to spread Christ's message. Saint Francis of Assisi founded the Franciscans, who have had a great influence in spreading the message throughout Europe. The Society of Jesus moved that message into parts of the world previously ignorant of Christ and his message. With the help of the Holy Spirit, the gospel is being preached in most corners of the world, as it will be until the end of time. Our ministry is to do our small part in the history of the world to share Christ's message.

✠ *What can I learn from this passage?*

Tribulation and confusion (24:15–28)

An old dictum says that God can write straight with crooked lines. The destruction of Jerusalem was tragic, but the resulting spread of the faith was a gift to other nations. When we pray, we do not always see how God answers our prayers until many years or decades later. Jesus calls us to pray with trust, whether we experience the answer to our prayer or others experience the answer many years later.

✠ *What can I learn from this passage?*

The coming of the Son of Man (24:29–31)

In reality, waiting for the end of the world is fruitless, since our life could easily end in an instant, and we will meet Christ long before the world ends. Jesus is foretelling the catastrophe to encourage us to be prepared for our entrance into eternity by living according to his message.

✠ *What can I learn from this passage?*

The lesson of the fig tree (24:32–35)

Jesus' words are eternal. His words to us come in the New Testament where we see the signs of Jesus' presence in the world. Our aim is to live in union with God's will as we would live it in heaven. Jesus' message will not pass away as long as there are Christians in the world who will keep it alive. In each of us, heaven and Earth meet as we attempt to fulfill God's will as we know it.

✠ *What can I learn from this passage?*

Be prepared (24:36–44)

An aspiring monk asked his abbot what he did every morning. The abbot told him he arose at five in the morning, prayed for an hour, ate breakfast, and went out in the field to work until noon. The young man then asked the abbot what he would do if he knew this would be his last day on Earth. The abbot answered that he would arise at five in the morning, pray for an hour, eat breakfast, and go out to work in the field. The story is another way of telling us that we should always be prepared for our last day on Earth, and it should be no different than any other day. We should always be ready when God calls.

✠ *What can I learn from this passage?*

PART 2: INDIVIDUAL STUDY (MATTHEW 24:45—25)

Through a series of parables, Jesus teaches the need to be vigilant and ready for the end of time. These parables, which speak of a master's returning unexpectedly from a trip, the foolish and wise virgins, the parable of the talents, and the judgment of the nations, teach about the end and the judgment that follows. This constitutes the second part of his eschatological discourse.

Day 1: The Faithful and Unfaithful Servant (24:45–51)

Jesus tells the story of a master who puts his servant in charge of his household. If the master returns unexpectedly and finds his servant has fulfilled his wishes well, he will reward him by putting him in charge of all his property. If, however, the master does not return for a period of time and the servant begins to misuse his property and beat the other servants, the master will severely punish the unfaithful servant. In this parable, Jesus warns us that although the end may not come immediately, we should always be prepared for the master's return. We are that servant put in charge of our part of the world.

Lectio Divina

Spend 8 to 10 minutes in silent contemplation of the following passage:

Remaining faithful to God in the midst of the temptations of life is difficult. Many remain faithful for a period of time, but when dryness strikes or the need to remain faithful to God's message becomes tedious or difficult, some begin to abandon God and live a life of sin and selfishness. We often hear of people who embraced their dedication to God with great enthusiasm and love but who later fell into sin for the sake of some pleasure or who simply later neglected any thought of God in their lives. We can expect moments of spiritual dryness, temptations to pleasure, or temptations to anger against God for some tragedy in life that makes us believe God is unfair. In the midst of these temptations, we pray the Master will come and find us to be faithful servants.

✠ *What can I learn from this passage?*

Day 2: The Parable of the Ten Virgins (25:1–13)

Jesus delivers a parable found only in this gospel. The idea of separation is already established as Jesus tells of five foolish and five wise virgins. In the time of Jesus, the groom would go to the home of the bride to meet with the girl's father and make the final arrangements for the marriage. Brief festivities would take place at the home of the bride, and then the bridegroom and bride would go in procession to the home of the groom. On his return to his home with his bride, the virgins would escort them to the groom's house for the wedding itself.

In Jesus' parable, the bridegroom took longer than expected, and the five foolish virgins did not have enough oil in their lamps to escort the bridegroom and bride to the groom's house. The wise virgins (wise to the end) decide they might not have enough oil to share with the unwise virgins, who then go to town to buy more oil. In their absence, the procession to the groom's house takes place, and the foolish virgins miss the wedding celebration.

The parable speaks of the final fulfillment of the kingdom. Although some belong to the reign of God, they are not well prepared for the Second Coming of Jesus. The message of the parable is clear. Jesus tells his audience to remain continually alert, because they do not know the day or the hour when he, the bridegroom, will come in glory.

Lectio Divina

Spend 8 to 10 minutes in silent contemplation of the following passage:

Not only is this a story of the end times, but it's a story with a ministry involved, namely, the ministry of the ten virgins who are to lead the bridegroom to the wedding. There are two types of faith: one is notional faith, and the other is real faith. Notional faith stops with what we are thinking, while real faith leads to action. The five foolish virgins have notional faith. They know they are to lead the bridegroom and bride from the home of the bride, but they foolishly do not prepare for a long wait. These are the people who have faith, but it wanes over time. Those with real faith keep the light of Christ alive in their hearts and remain faithful to the end.

✠ *What can I learn from this passage?*

Day 3: The Parable of the Talents (25:14–30)

The parable of the talents speaks of the proper use of the gifts God gives us. The master (the Son of Man) is going away on a trip, and he gives a large amount of money (talents) to each of his slaves. When he returns unexpectedly, he finds that two of the servants have used the talents well and have doubled the amount given. The master, pleased with the servants, gives them greater wealth and responsibility and invites them to share in the "master's joy" (eternal life). The third slave, fearing he would lose the talent he received, did nothing with it. The master is angry with this servant; he deals with him harshly and gives the servant's only talent to the successful servants. This third servant had hoarded his talent, not even depositing it so that it could be used by others. Jesus is telling his audience that the disciple who uses the gifts given by God will receive more in return, whereas the person who does not use the gifts given by God will lose whatever gift he or she has received. Like the master in the story, Jesus demands much of those with whom he shares his gifts.

Lectio Divina

Spend 8 to 10 minutes in silent contemplation of the following passage:

Many people who read the parable of the talents feel the master was unfair in giving only one talent to the third man while giving more to the first two. The story concerns the use of talents, not the amount. A cardinal who becomes pope may receive more talents, but that does not necessarily mean he will receive a greater reward than the one who picks grapes for a living. God gives talents and expects us to use them for God's greater honor and glory.

✠ *What can I learn from this passage?*

Day 4: The Judgment of the Nations (25:31–46)

Matthew presents an apocalyptic picture of Jesus, the Son of Man, escorted by angels and sitting on his royal throne. The passage concerns the Final Judgment and again speaks of separating one group from another. During Jesus' time, the sheep and the goats often grazed together during the day but were separated at night. Jesus refers to the good as the sheep and the bad as the goats. In this passage, all nations appear before the Son of Man to face their judgment. Those who feed the hungry, give drink to the thirsty, welcome the stranger, clothe the naked, and visit those in prison are the sheep who will inherit the kingdom (eternal life) prepared for them. Those who do not do these virtuous acts, the goats, will be condemned. Jesus identifies himself with the "least ones," which could refer to the Christians or to all those people in need. This identification of Jesus with the least ones reflects the thinking of the early Church community for whom Matthew wrote his gospel.

Lectio Divina

Spend 8 to 10 minutes in silent contemplation of the following passage:

> When Jesus speaks to the sheep and the goats about feeding the hungry, giving drink to the thirsty, welcoming the stranger, clothing the naked, caring for those who are ill, and visiting those who are in prison, both ask when they did or did not do this. Neither of them saw Jesus, but Jesus proclaims the way they treated others was the way they treated him. The same judgment will fall upon us. The manner in which we treat others is the manner in which we treat Christ.

✠ *What can I learn from this passage?*

Review Questions

1. Who are the faithful and unfaithful servants?
2. What is the message of the ten virgins?
3. What is the message of the talents?
4. What message does Jesus teach when he speaks of the sheep and the goats?

The Passion and Resurrection

MATTHEW 26–28

Go, therefore, and make disciples of all nations, baptizing them in the name of the Father, and of the Son, and of the holy Spirit, teaching them to observe all that I have commanded you. And behold, I am with you always, until the end of the age (28:19–20).

Opening Prayer (SEE PAGE 14)

Context

Part 1: Matthew 26 The author employs a major portion of the Passion narrative of Mark in his presentation of the passion and death of Jesus. He uses the prediction of Jesus' impending death by crucifixion as a transition from the parables on the kingdom to the Passion narrative. Matthew presents Jesus as having full control of the situation and full knowledge of his death. From the conspiracy against Jesus to his trial before the Sanhedrin and Peter's denial, Jesus stands firm while the weaknesses of Jesus' disciples become dominant.

Part 2: Matthew 27—28 Jesus' passion, death, and resurrection become dominant in a fast-moving depiction of Jesus' agonizing journey to the cross, his crucifixion, and his final triumph in his resurrection. The passage ends with Jesus' command to his disciples to make disciples of all nations and to baptize them in the name of the Father, and of the Son, and of the Holy Spirit. The gospel reaches its climax by linking the final event with Matthew's infancy narrative. Jesus declares he will be with his disciples always, until the end of the age. He is again Emmanuel, "God with us."

PART 1: GROUP STUDY (MATTHEW 26)

Read aloud Matthew 26

26:1–5 The conspiracy against Jesus

Jesus calmly predicts that he will be handed over in just two days, when the Passover is celebrated. In contrast to the calm shown by Jesus, the chief priests and the elders meet with the high priest, Caiaphas, to secretly plot against Jesus. The contradictions found in this Passion narrative begin here. In this passage, the chief priests and elders decide not to arrest Jesus during the feast lest the crowds riot, but as we shall see later in Matthew, they actually do arrest him during the feast.

26:6–16 The anointing at Bethany

A woman anoints Jesus with expensive perfume at the home of Simon the leper, a person otherwise unknown to us today. The woman is not identified by name, although Jesus promises that the deed will not be forgotten. The disciples' objection to this wasteful use of oil shows their lack of understanding concerning Jesus' coming death. Because of the type of death Jesus must face, there won't be time to anoint his body. This "anointing" by the woman prepares Jesus for his burial.

Matthew (as well as Mark) gives no motive for Judas's betrayal of Jesus, but Matthew does add that Jesus was betrayed for thirty pieces of silver. The amount of the payment recalls the prophecy of Zechariah (11:12), who spoke of a discarded shepherd receiving a wage of thirty silver pieces. Matthew could be telling us that the religious leaders saw Jesus as worth no more than this. Judas now awaits his opportunity to betray Jesus.

26:17–30 Events at the Passover

Matthew shortens Mark's account (14:12–16) of the preparation of the Passover meal. The expressed longing of Jesus to share this meal reflects its importance. Just as Judas awaits an opportune time to betray Jesus, so Jesus awaits his "appointed time." The events surrounding the preparation of the meal also point to the meal's importance.

Jesus continues to show his control of the situation as he announces that one of his disciples will betray him. Each disciple expresses his own insecurity by asking if he is the one. During a meal, it was customary to dip bread into a common dish and even to pass the bread to another as a friendly gesture. Jesus uses this action to share that he knows Judas is his betrayer. Although Jesus was destined to die this way (according to the Scriptures), it does not lessen the guilt of the one who betrays him. The intensity of the betrayal is shown by the fact that Judas, his betrayer, is sharing the intimacy of the meal with Jesus. Matthew shows the faith of the other disciples who address Jesus by the title of "Lord," while Judas, who lacks faith, addresses Jesus as "Rabbi." Jesus allows Judas's own words to condemn him.

The description of the eucharistic meal makes use of liturgical ritual followed at the time of the writing of the gospel. Jesus takes bread, blesses it, breaks it, and gives it to his disciples with the words that they should "take, eat," and "drink from it." The idea of the bread and wine given as the Body and Blood of Jesus links the meal with the death of Jesus that is about to take place. The words "blood of the covenant" recall an event in the Book of Exodus (24:8) in which Moses sprinkled the people with blood as a sign of entering a covenant. Matthew quotes from Isaiah (53:12) when he states that the blood will be shed on behalf of many, and he adds the final phrase, "for the forgiveness of sins."

Jesus ends by telling his disciples that he will not drink of the wine again until he drinks it with them in the Father's kingdom. The fact that Jesus emphasizes the "Father's" kingdom and not his own seems to imply that Jesus will not take part in this cup until the end of time, when his Father's kingdom reaches fulfillment. Jesus and his disciples end the meal with the customary singing of hymns. They leave for the Mount of Olives, where they intend to stay for the evening.

26:31–35 Peter's denial foretold

Jesus warns his disciples that their faith will be shaken that evening, and he quotes Zechariah (13:7), who foretold that the sheep would scatter when the shepherd is struck. Jesus offers them hope by telling them about his resurrection and that he will go before them into Galilee. Peter boasts of his dedication to Jesus, and Jesus warns him that he will deny Jesus three times before the cock crows. Peter vows to die with Jesus if necessary, and the others boast the same.

26:36–46 The Agony in the Garden

As Jesus withdraws to pray at Gethsemane, he takes Peter, James, and John with him. The presence of these three disciples, who also accompanied Jesus at the time of the transfiguration, underlines the importance of this moment. Jesus tells of his great sorrow and asks his disciples to remain awake with him. The struggle in the garden shows Jesus' agony and his human conflict with the passion he must undergo, and it shows the lack of understanding, as well as the weakness, of the disciples of Jesus. Despite his great fear, Jesus accepts the call of God's will. On his third return to the sleeping disciples, Jesus awakens them because the betrayer has arrived. Jesus openly accepts that the appointed hour has come when he must be "handed over" to the power of evil.

26:47–56 The betrayal and arrest of Jesus

Judas leads a large crowd sent out by the chief priests and elders. The infamy of Judas' betrayal is heightened as Matthew calls him "one of the Twelve." This intimacy with Jesus allows him to use a sign of friendship to point out Jesus to the crowd. Judas embraces Jesus and calls him by the title used by those who do not have faith in Jesus; he addresses him as "Rabbi." Jesus orders Judas to do what he came to do.

One of Jesus' companions, identified as Peter in the Gospel of John, cuts off the ear of the high priest's servant. Jesus warns that the use of the sword will lead to death by the sword. Matthew continues to show that Jesus is in control of the situation. He could have heavenly help if he wished, but this was the moment the Scriptures had foretold, when the suffering and death of the servant Jesus was to reach its fulfillment. Jesus reminds the crowd that they could have taken him at any time when he openly preached in the Temple, but this was the way it had to be done to fulfill the Scriptures. As predicted earlier by Jesus, the disciples desert him.

26:57–68 Jesus before the Sanhedrin

Matthew follows Mark's Gospel closely. Jesus is led to the house of the high priest Caiaphas, where the scribes and elders had come together to judge Jesus. Matthew also mirrors Mark by contrasting the unfaltering dedication of Jesus with the weakness of Peter. As Jesus is brought into the house, Peter sits outside with the guards. Jewish Law forbids a night trial, and some commentators see Jesus' trial in the house of Caiaphas as an attempt to gain evidence for a formal condemnation at daybreak.

Although the evidence against Jesus is contradictory, two witnesses accuse him of claiming he could destroy the Temple and rebuild it in three days. The assembly accepts their testimony. The reader of the gospel in the early Church would immediately recognize that Jesus was speaking of the temple of his own body, which would be destroyed through the crucifixion and raised on the third day.

Jesus shows respect for the authority of the high priest when he orders Jesus to tell them under oath whether he is the Messiah, the Son of God. The addition of the title "Son of God" was more likely put on the lips of the high priest by the preaching of the early Church. Because the Israelites did not expect the Messiah to be divine, the high priest would not have thought of asking Jesus such a question. Jesus answers that it is the high priest himself who says this about him being the Messiah. When Jesus tells the high priest that he will see the Son of Man (Jesus) seated at the right hand of the Power (God) and coming on the clouds of heaven, the high priest rips his garments, a dramatic sign that one has just heard blasphemy. The others join with the high priest in proclaiming that Jesus has blasphemed, and they cry out that he deserves death. The acts of spitting, slapping, and ridicule may have been added by the author to show the religious leaders' contempt for Jesus. It seems unlikely they would have acted this way.

26:69–75 Peter denies Jesus

The scene now turns to Peter, who must face his accusers concerning his relationship with Jesus. The servant girls and the bystanders accuse Peter of being with Jesus, and he denies it. As each group accuses Peter of being with Jesus, he denies it. On his third denial, the cock crows. Peter remembers Jesus' prediction and weeps bitterly. Jesus faces his accusers with courage and honesty; Peter faces his with cowardice and lies. The members of the early Church who had denied Christ at some stressful moment must have found some comfort in the fact that even Peter, the great apostle, had his own moments of weakness.

Review Questions

1. What is significant about the anointing of Jesus at Bethany?
2. How did Judas help the religious leaders in plotting to capture Jesus?
3. What happened at the Last Supper?
4. What happened during Jesus' agony in the garden?
5. What is significant about Jesus' appearance before the Sanhedrin?
6. What happened when Peter denied Jesus?

Closing Prayer (SEE PAGE 14)

Pray the closing prayer now or after *lectio divina*.

Lectio Divina (SEE PAGE 7)

Relax your body and maintain a posture of prayer (back straight, eyes shut, feet flat on the floor). This exercise can take as long as you want, but in the context of this Bible study, 10 to 20 minutes should be sufficient.

The meditations that follow are provided only to help group participants use this prayer form, but note that *lectio* is intended to bring one to a place of prayerful contemplation where the Word of God speaks to the hearer from his or her heart. (See page 7 for further instruction.)

The conspiracy against Jesus (26:1–5)

The chief priests and elders are less concerned about the religious festival that is about to take place than they are about getting rid of Jesus. Like many of us, the religious leaders are easily distracted from an important religious event while Jesus does not overlook the need to celebrate the central feast of Judaism, even in the face of his impending crucifixion.

✠ *What can I learn from this passage?*

The anointing at Bethany (26:6–16)

An action that seemed a useless waste of money becomes an important event in Jesus' life, so important that Jesus promises the woman's action of anointing him will be remembered in the preaching of the gospel. When we reach out to others, we may never know until eternity how important it was.

✠ *What can I learn from this passage?*

Events at the Passover (26:17–30)

During the celebration of the Eucharist, some could be betraying Jesus by hurting others in the community or by bearing false witness against them. Jesus offers us his Body and Blood and welcomes those who betray him to dine with him. In our celebration of the Eucharist, there is no room for judging others.

✠ *What can I learn from this passage?*

Peter's denial foretold (26:31–35)

When we celebrate a sacrament, we are protesting that, like Peter, if all abandon Christ, we will not; but then comes the test. At the celebration of the sacrament of baptism, we commit our lives to Christ, and we renew that commitment each time we celebrate Eucharist. But many of us fail and betray Christ by sin and by not living up to our promise. Peter becomes our comfort in moments such as that. Peter, who can boast that he will never betray Christ, shows how weak he is but also how repentant he can be.

✠ *What can I learn from this passage?*

The Agony in the Garden (26:36–46)

The Church asks us to spend one hour a week with the Christian community in our worship of God. Some escape before the hour ends, anxious to get out of the parking lot or get to a restaurant. Jesus asks for only an hour, and we must examine how we respond.

✠ *What can I learn from this passage?*

The betrayal and arrest of Jesus (26:47–56)

Jesus came in peace. Because this is the appointed time, he does not call upon heavenly powers to help him but faces his impending passion with courage. Like Jesus, Christians should share Jesus' message in a peaceful manner.

✠ *What can I learn from this passage?*

Jesus before the Sanhedrin (26:57–68)

A man in prison for driving under the influence of alcohol told a reporter that prison life was difficult, but the hardest thing about being accused of the crime was the loneliness of having all his friends abandon him. Matthew tells us that when the crowd took Jesus before the Sanhedrin, Peter followed at a distance, as did his other disciples. Jesus had to suffer his passion alone. Jesus, who knew he would experience the loneliness of someone being accused of a crime, urged us earlier in Matthew's Gospel to visit the lonely, the sick, and the imprisoned who were often abandoned by friends they expected to support them in times of need. We need not follow Jesus at a distance.

✠ *What can I learn from this passage?*

Peter denies Jesus (26:69–75)

Peter, a close friend of Jesus who denied even knowing him, had the need to have a greater debt forgiven. As we know, Jesus forgave Peter, but it was a denial Peter could never forget. We all realize that no matter how badly any of us may have sinned, forgiveness is always present when we seek it.

✠ *What can I learn from this passage?*

PART 2: INDIVIDUAL STUDY (MATTHEW 27—28)

The passion, death, and resurrection in Matthew's Gospel reach their climax when Jesus comes before Pilate. Now the whole of Jerusalem is involved: a Roman ruler, the religious leaders, and the people. The tragedy leads to the joy of the resurrection. In these passages we arrive at the Good News of Jesus Christ, where we can proclaim with a centurion, "Truly, this was the Son of God."

Day 1: Jesus Before Pilate (27:1–10)

The formal and legal action taken by the religious leaders against Jesus occurs at daybreak. Jesus is brought before Pilate, who as procurator, is in Jerusalem to keep the peace during the Passover. Matthew interrupts his narrative about Jesus to speak about the remorse and despair of Judas. This passage is found only in the Gospel of Matthew.

Matthew describes a remorseful Judas taking the silver pieces back to the chief priests and elders and then going off to hang himself. The suicide of Judas found in the Gospel of Matthew differs from that found in the Acts of the Apostles (1:18). In Acts, Judas falls headfirst into a field. The chief priests decide they cannot use "blood money" for the Temple treasury, so they use it to buy a field for the burial of the poor. They unwittingly, according to Matthew, fulfill an Old Testament prophecy from Jeremiah, which tells of thirty pieces of silver (as the price on a man's head) that was later used to buy a potter's field. The prophecy is actually an accumulation of many prophecies. (See Zechariah 11:13; Jeremiah 18:2–3, 19:1–2, 32:15.)

Lectio Divina

Spend 8 to 10 minutes in silent contemplation of the following passage:

> In contrast to Peter who wept bitterly over his denial but did not despair of Jesus' forgiveness, Judas in his despair hanged himself. In reading the events of Jesus' passion and death, we know Jesus would have forgiven him if he'd repented, but Judas did not have Peter's faith. He hanged himself because he'd betrayed an innocent man. The episode reminds us that Jesus will forgive our sins no mat-

ter how grave, but we must trust Jesus and seek forgiveness. God is willing to forgive, but forgiveness must be accepted.

✠ *What can I learn from this passage?*

Day 2: Jesus Questioned and Sentenced by Pilate (27:11–26)

When Jesus appears before Pilate, Pilate asks him if he is the "king of the Jews." Because the religious leaders brought Jesus before the Roman tribunal, they want to accuse him of a crime against the empire. The claim of being the king of the Jews would certainly be a crime worthy of the death penalty. Jesus answers Pilate in the same way he answered the high priest in an earlier confrontation; he states that Pilate is the one who makes this accusation. Jesus realizes Pilate can never fully understand the meaning of the title. Jesus remains silent when Pilate asks him about the charges brought against him. His silence recalls the words of Isaiah (53:7), who foretold that the Suffering Servant would remain silent in his suffering. Although history shows Pilate was not a sympathetic and weak person, Matthew depicts him as a man intent upon releasing Jesus.

The reference to an ancient custom of releasing a prisoner on the feast is found only in the gospels. Pilate, recognizing the jealousy of the religious leaders over the popularity of Jesus, asks if they want Barabbas or Jesus. Meanwhile, the wife of Pilate has a dream about Jesus, "that innocent man," and she warns Pilate to have nothing to do with him. Just as dreams provide messages about Jesus in the early chapters of the Gospel of Matthew, so a dream provides a final message here. The people, influenced by the religious leaders, cry out to Pilate to release Barabbas and to crucify Jesus. Pilate, fearing a riot, symbolically washes his hands of guilt and passes the burden of guilt onto the crowd, which loudly accepts it for themselves and their children. These words, taken literally throughout the centuries, have sadly and mistakenly led some Christians to persecute the Jews. Matthew, conscious of the destruction of Jerusalem, may have seen this tragedy as God's answer to the Jewish clamor for Jesus' life. As was customary with those condemned to death, Jesus is first scourged.

Lectio Divina

Spend 8 to 10 minutes in silent contemplation of the following passage:

> A man who worked long and hard for a politician whom he later found to be taking bribes from a company working in his city told a friend, "I washed my hands of him." When the people clamored for the crucifixion of Jesus, Pilate washed his hands of Jesus. When we sin, we may not use the expression of washing our hands of Jesus, but for that moment and that act, we are in fact doing so. We can understand the impact of sin when we realize that, like Pilate, we are washing our hands of Jesus.

✠ *What can I learn from this passage?*

Day 3: The Passion of Jesus (27:27–44)

The custom of mocking a rebel from among the Jews as a false aspirant to the throne could have been Rome's way of treating any leader of an uprising, and it could have been used for people other than Jesus. In Jesus' case, however, the mockery unwittingly contained words of truth. The soldiers put a crown of thorns on Jesus' head and a royal robe on his shoulders, and they mocked him by hailing him as the "king of the Jews." Jesus was truly the king of the Jews and all people. After they mocked and abused Jesus, they put his own clothes on him and led him off to crucifixion. Matthew says little about the journey to the cross except that a man named Simon of Cyrene is forced to help Jesus carry the cross. This could have been done to ensure that Jesus would live to suffer the cruel death of crucifixion.

The soldiers crucify Jesus at a place called Golgotha, a name which means "Skull Place" (possibly because the shape of the hill resembled a skull). Jesus, like the prophets, dies outside the holy city of Jerusalem. The soldiers divide his garments by casting lots, as foretold in the Psalms (22:19). Ironically, the plaque above Jesus' head tauntingly reads "King of the Jews." This recalls the mockery foretold in Psalm 22:7–8. The thieves crucified on either side of Jesus, the people passing by, the chief priests, the scribes, and the elders all join in to mock Jesus. The crowd challenges Jesus to use his miraculous powers to save himself. The challenge recalls the words of Satan in the desert at the outset of Jesus' ministry when Satan tries to lure Jesus into proving he is the Son of God by performing miracles and having God save him from a leap from the highest point in the Temple. Just as Jesus did not respond to that temptation to use his powers for his own sake in the desert, so he refuses to use them in the midst of his passion.

Lectio Divina

Spend 8 to 10 minutes in silent contemplation of the following passage:

> To understand God's love, we must let the most important act of creation sink into our hearts; the Son of God not only became human, but he actually suffered and died for us. God could have chosen another time in history when death could have been painless and swift, such as we have in our own era in many countries. But the Son of God endured a slow, agonizing death. At any moment he could have called upon heavenly help to ease the pain and free him from this life, but he did not. What more can we say about God's love for us?

✠ *What can I learn from this passage?*

Day 4: The Death of Jesus (27:45–56)

For three hours, Jesus hung upon the cross under a cloak of darkness. This darkness, which symbolizes the cover of evil, sends its shadow across the whole Earth. Jesus cries out with the first words from Psalm 22, "My God, my God, why have you abandoned me?" The words show the pain and despair of Jesus, but they also offer some hope for rescue, as found at the end of Psalm 22. There was a legend among the Jews that Elijah would save prisoners from the cruelty of the Romans. Some mistake Jesus' prayer as a call to Elijah for help. The wine offered to Jesus was a mild mixture meant to alleviate some of his pain. Matthew tells his readers that Jesus "breathed his last."

The Earth responds in chaos to Jesus' death. The curtain of the Temple is torn in two at the moment Jesus dies, thus throwing open the Holy of Holies to the whole world and demonstrating the end of the Old Covenant. Matthew adds some apocalyptic elements that heighten the significance of

Jesus' death. The Earth quakes, boulders split, the tombs of the dead open, and the dead are raised. The centurion and his men, as representatives of the Gentile people, declare, "Truly, this was the Son of God!" Many people from the Gentile nations would profess that same faith in Jesus in the years ahead. The only faithful witnesses mentioned are the women who have followed Jesus from Galilee and who now look upon the crucifixion from a distance.

Lectio Divina

Spend 8 to 10 minutes in silent contemplation of the following passage:

> When we want to show love for others, we use our funds to buy gifts for them, we visit them in their illness, we perform tasks they are not able to do, or we perform other deeds allowed by our health and power. But the wisdom of Jesus taught us another type of power. In the midst of our suffering, we can say to another, "I am offering up this pain for you." To many, this would sound foolish, but to God, it is wisdom. Jesus suffered and died for us, and he taught us that there is value in offering up our suffering and dying for others.

✠ *What can I learn from this passage?*

Day 5: The Burial of Jesus (27:57–66)

Joseph of Arimathea, a disciple of Jesus and a wealthy man, requests the body of Jesus to bury it. Pilate releases the body to Joseph, who wraps it in fresh linen and lays it in a new tomb cut from the rocks around Jerusalem. A huge stone is rolled across the entrance. Because there were many burial places surrounding the walls of Jerusalem, Mary Magdalene and the other Mary make special note of the place of the burial. The religious leaders, recalling Jesus' prediction of resurrection on the third day, ask Pilate to place a guard at the tomb. Pilate refuses, and the religious leaders set their own guard. The religious leaders fear the disciples of Jesus may come and steal his body. In reality, the chief priests would not have concerned themselves with such predictions. The events surrounding the burial of Jesus are mentioned to emphasize that Jesus is really dead and that many people have witnessed his death. Matthew leaves the reader with little doubt that

Jesus was truly dead and securely buried in a grave, the location of which only a few knew. This sets the stage for the resurrection of Jesus.

Lectio Divina

Spend 8 to 10 minutes in silent contemplation of the following passage:

> Shortly before his assassination, Oscar Romero, an archbishop in El Salvador, told a reporter, "You can tell the people that if they succeed in killing me, that I forgive and bless those who do it. Hopefully, they will realize they are wasting their time. A bishop will die, but the Church of God, which is the people, will never perish." In Jesus' case, the religious leaders hope to silence Jesus by his passion and death, but instead, his ordeal would eventually become known to the world, and their misdeeds would also become known. Since Jesus' day, the voices of good people who have suffered and died for the rights of the people whom God loves have been heard loud and clear through history. Evil can kill a person, but not the good that person does. The burial of Jesus was a burial of his body, not his message.

> ✠ *What can I learn from this passage?*

Day 6: Resurrection of Jesus and the Commissioning of the Disciples (28:1–20)

The resurrection narrative found in the Gospel of Matthew includes the story of the empty tomb and only one appearance of Jesus. Matthew names two women, Mary Magdalene and the other Mary, as coming to the tomb. These are the same women who witnessed the burial of Jesus and who could testify that the events occurred at the place where Jesus was buried. Matthew's Gospel alone presents witnesses to the removal of the stone. He makes use of apocalyptic language as he speaks of an earthquake and an angel from heaven who resembled a flash of lightning and whose clothing was white as snow. The guards also witness this event and become paralyzed with fear. The angel identifies Jesus as the one who was crucified and who is not there.

The resurrection story does not deal immediately with the presence of

Jesus, but rather with the absence of Jesus, namely, the empty tomb. Jesus has been raised as he had foretold three times throughout his ministry. The angel calls the women to witness the place of the burial, and then tells them to go to the disciples and tell them that Jesus, as he foretold before his death, has gone on before them to Galilee, where they will see him. On their way to the disciples, the women meet Jesus. He greets them and tells the women to give the word to the disciples that he is going on to Galilee, where he will meet them.

During the period in which Matthew wrote his gospel, a rumor apparently hinted that the disciples of Jesus had stolen his body and that he was not really raised from the dead. The story of the soldiers accepting a bribe to spread this rumor becomes important to the Gospel of Matthew. It seems unlikely that soldiers who had experienced such an event as described at the tomb could so easily be bribed to spread the tale that the body of Jesus had been stolen.

These final verses not only bring the Gospel of Matthew to an end, but they also sum up the message of the gospel. The mission of Jesus, begun in Israel, now moves out to the whole world. The disciples of Jesus come to an unnamed mountain to which Jesus has called them. The name of the mountain is not as important as the events that take place there, the place of God's heavenly visitation to the people. Just as the astrologers paid homage to the infant in the infancy narratives, the disciples now pay homage to Jesus as the resurrected Christ.

Jesus speaks his message to the Eleven. He has received full authority from the Father, an authority that reaches into our own world and into eternity. The Eleven are told to go out and make disciples of all nations. By this time, the reader of the Gospel of Matthew has become familiar with the implications of discipleship. The disciples are no longer confined to Israel, but they must go out to "all the nations." They are to baptize in the name of the Father, and of the Son, and of the Holy Spirit. This was a baptismal formula used by the community in which Matthew wrote his gospel. We learn in this formula that God is one. We do not baptize "in the names of," but "in the name of," recalling that the Father, Son, and Holy Spirit constitute the one true God. The disciples must teach all nations the message Jesus taught them.

The Gospel of Matthew ends with the encouraging words that Jesus will be with his Church always, until the end of the world. Matthew makes no mention of the ascension of Jesus.

Lectio Divina

Spend 8 to 10 minutes in silent contemplation of the following passage:

The resurrection and ascension of Jesus are central teachings of Christianity. Jesus' passion and death would not have been enough to bring salvation. Evil would have conquered if it had not been for the resurrection. The gospel ends as Jesus commissions the Eleven to go out and make disciples of all nations. We are part of that mission, called to share Christ's message and to lead people to be baptized in the name of the Father, and of the Son, and of the Holy Spirit. We live our Christian life with the final words of Matthew's Gospel as words of great encouragement: "And behold, I am with you always, until the end of the age." Jesus, the Christ, the Son of God, is Emmanuel, God with us until the end of time.

✠ *What can I learn from this passage?*

Review Questions

1. Why did the Sanhedrin need Pilate to condemn Jesus to death?
2. Why did Pilate seem to plead for the life of Jesus?
3. What was ironic about the manner in which the soldiers mocked Jesus?
4. What happened when Jesus died?